ROUTLEDGE LIBRARY EDITIONS:
BANKING & FINANCE

THE MORTGAGE MARKET

THE MORTGAGE MARKET

MARK BOLÉAT AND
ADRIAN COLES

Volume 2

Routledge
Taylor & Francis Group
LONDON AND NEW YORK

First published in 1987

This edition first published in 2012
by Routledge
4 Park Square, Milton Park, Abingdon, Oxon OX14 4RN
605 Third Avenue, New York, NY 10017

Routledge is an imprint of the Taylor & Francis Group, an informa business

British Library Cataloguing in Publication Data
A catalogue record for this book is available from the British Library

ISBN: 978-0-415-52086-7 (Set)
ISBN: 978-0-203-10819-2 (ebk) (Set)
ISBN: 978-0-415-53787-2 (hbk)(Volume 2)
ISBN: 978-0-203-10996-0 (ebk) (Volume 2)

Publisher's Note
The publisher has gone to great lengths to ensure the quality of this reprint but points out that some imperfections in the original copies may be apparent.

The Mortgage Market

Mark Boléat and Adrian Coles

LONDON
ALLEN & UNWIN
Boston Sydney Wellington

Allen & Unwin, the academic imprint of
Unwin Hyman Ltd
PO Box 18, Park Lane, Hemel Hempstead, Herts HP2 4TE, UK
40 Museum Street, London WC1A 1LU, UK
37/39 Queen Elizabeth Street, London SE1 2QB, UK

Allen & Unwin Inc.,
8 Winchester Place, Winchester, Mass. 01890, USA

Allen & Unwin (Australia) Ltd,
8 Napier Street, North Sydney, NSW 2060, Australia

Allen & Unwin (New Zealand) Ltd in association with
the Port Nicholson Press Ltd,
60 Cambridge Terrace, Wellington, New Zealand

First published in 1987

British Library Cataloguing in Publication Data

Boléat, Mark
The mortgage market. — (Studies in financial institutions and markets; 3)
1. Mortgage loans — Great Britain 2. Housing — Great Britain
I. Title II. Coles, Adrian III. Series
339.4'8332722'0941 HG2040.5.G7
ISBN 0-04-334011-3

Library of Congress Cataloging in Publication Data

Boléat, Mark.
The mortgage market
(Studies in financial institutions and markets; 3)
Bibliography: p. Includes index
1. Mortgage loans—Great Britain. 2. Housing—Great Britain—Finance. 3. Financial institutions—Great Britain. I. Coles, Adrian, 1954–
II. Title. III. Series
HG2040.5.G7B65 1987 332.7'22 86-28875
ISBN 0-04-334011-3 (alk. paper)

Set in 10 on 11 point Plantin by Fotographics (Bedford) Ltd
and printed in Great Britain by Billing and Sons Ltd, London and Worcester

Contents

Contents

List of Figures and Tables

Figures

Tables

Preface

The mortgage market in Britain is changing rapidly. A few years ago building societies had a near monopoly of mortgage finance, and the market was characterized by a shortage of funds. Now banks, building societies and a number of non-traditional institutions are competing aggressively for mortgage business.

This book analyses mortgage markets in a theoretical context, covering, in particular, recent market developments and major policy issues in Britain.

The first part discusses the relationship between housing tenure and housing finance, and then the relationship between housing finance and financial intermediation. The second part analyses the four types of housing finance system: the informal system, the deposit-taking system, the mortgage bank system and the contract system. Part III analyses the British housing finance market. Chapters cover government policies towards the market, loan terms and instruments, the evolution of a competitive mortgage market and the emergence of securitization. Part IV considers three major policy issues: housing finance and the real economy, housing subsidies and the internationalization of housing finance. The one chapter in Part V looks at future trends in owner-occupation and housing finance.

The authors are grateful to their employers, The Building Societies Association, for permitting them to write this book and for allowing them to draw so freely on the Association's resources. They gratefully acknowledge the assistance given by Janet Perkins, Julie Patrick and Sharon Barnett in preparing the text so willingly and competently. Janet Perkins, Mark Boléat's secretary, was largely responsible for preparing successive drafts of the book. Julie Patrick, Adrian Coles's secretary, and Sharon Barnett shared this work, particularly at the later stages.

Mark Boléat
Adrian Coles
London, 1986

PART I

Introduction

1 Housing Tenure and Housing Finance

This book is concerned with the finance of owner-occupation, and it is therefore helpful to begin with a brief analysis of types of housing tenure and patterns of tenure, comparing the position in Britain with that in the rest of the world. This chapter also includes a discussion of the relationship between housing tenure, which can be regarded as a real economic variable, and finance for house purchase, which is a monetary variable. Obviously the two variables are linked, but, as will be shown in this and the next chapter, the links are somewhat tenuous, with the housing finance market being more affected by fiscal and monetary factors than by housing factors.

Types of Housing Tenure

There are two basic forms of housing tenure: owner-occupation and renting. In simple terms the owner-occupier owns the dwelling in which he lives while the tenant has an agreement to occupy the dwelling, perhaps for a limited time, for which he pays rent to the owner. While this broad categorization is sufficient for many purposes, including for this book, it should be noted that within the two categories there are a number of sub-divisions, and at the margin the dividing line between owner-occupation and renting is blurred. Moreover, the characteristics of owner-occupation in one country may not apply in others, and, indeed, the perverse situation can occur of owner-occupation in one country having the characteristics of renting in another and vice versa.

In most industrialized countries owner-occupied, single-family dwellings and flats or apartments have slightly different forms of legal tenure. For single-family dwellings, including terraced and semi-detached houses, there are generally no shared parts, and therefore no problem in the owner-occupier owning the land on which the dwelling stands, nor, in the normal course of events, does the occupier have to share any services with his neighbours. In Britain the vast majority of owner-occupiers in single-family dwellings own their dwellings freehold, meaning they own the land on which their houses are built. However, in some parts of the country (notably South Wales) some single-family units are owned on long leases with a fairly small ground rent being paid to the owner of the land. For most practical purposes this form of tenure is identical to freehold tenure and often it is possible for the owner of a long leasehold house to purchase the freehold.

Flats cannot be owned in the same way because provision has to be made for the maintenance of the common parts. The normal arrangement in Britain is for flats to be owned on a leasehold basis, the lease initially running perhaps for 99 years or in some cases 999 years. The owner of a flat pays a ground rent and service charge to the landlord. The owner is free to sell his interest in the flat at any time and thus can benefit from any capital appreciation. This is therefore clearly owner-occupation although the owners of such dwellings have less control over their homes than do those living in self-contained units. Moreover, as the lease approaches the expiry date, so the property will begin to lose value and ultimately ownership will return to the owner of the land. It is difficult in Britain to obtain a mortgage loan to purchase a leasehold property unless the lease has at least twenty years to run beyond the mortgage term.

In other countries – Australia, the USA and Sweden, for example – many owner-occupied flats are held in a different way by which the owners of the flats jointly own the common parts. This removes many of the disadvantages of the leasehold form of tenure, such as the owner of the land often not properly fulfilling his responsibilities as landlord, and also the problem of depreciating leases as the leasehold term expires. The system is called 'strata title' in Australia, 'condominiums' in the USA, and 'tenant ownership' in Sweden. This form of tenure is nearer to full owner-occupation than the British leasehold system.

Rented housing is generally quite distinct from owner-occupied housing in that the tenant has no right to any of the capital appreciation of the dwelling, and generally no responsibility for the maintenance of the structure. However, this is not always the case. In Britain expensive flats are sometimes made available on short leases with a fairly modest rent, but a substantial premium has to be paid to acquire the lease. When the lease has been acquired it can then subsequently be sold and the owner of such a lease can be regarded in some senses as an owner-occupier. However, this is partly a consequence of legislation with respect to rented housing and the tax system. Mortgage finance is generally not available to purchase a lease of this type.

Recently, hybrid schemes have been introduced in Britain which combine elements of both renting and owner-occupation. Housing co-operatives come into this category. These are schemes by which participants jointly own all of the dwellings and jointly participate in the capital appreciation. However, the individual dwellings are rented from the co-operative. Shared ownership schemes are another hybrid category. Under these a person purchases part of a dwelling while simultaneously paying rent on the remainder; at a later stage (or stages) he is able to acquire the rented part. This is seen as being an easy entry into owner-occupation and a number of such schemes have been developed in Britain in recent years, generally with housing associations or local authorities owning the rented part.

In Britain it is accepted that one of the characteristics of owner-occupation is that the owner is free to sell the dwelling to anyone he wishes. This is not the case throughout the world. Hungary provides an interesting contrast. Although there is a high level of owner-occupation, higher than in Britain, often an owner-occupier can sell only with the consent of the local authority. Moreover, to acquire rented housing it is often necessary to pay a premium and it follows that the occupier can benefit from any capital appreciation. This is a cautionary note when making international comparisons.

Notwithstanding these various complications, it is still generally the case that there is a fairly sharp division between owner-occupation and renting. Basically owner-occupation means that the occupier benefits fully from any capital appreciation (and similarly faces the risk, generally low in Britain, of capital depreciation), and is able to obtain a loan secured on the house by way of a mortgage to purchase it. This obviously applies to single-family dwellings, but also to flats, acquired on a leasehold basis in Britain or on a condominium-type basis in other countries.

Housing Tenure: Theoretical Considerations

Before considering statistics on owner-occupation it is helpful to analyse on a theoretical basis the demand for particular types of housing tenure, and therefore the patterns of housing tenure which one would expect to exist both within countries and between countries. This theoretical analysis can be considered by reference to major variables, in particular, wealth, age and location.

In Britain it seems to be accepted that owner-occupation is associated with wealth and certainly the statistics show that the richer people are, the more likely they are to be owner-occupiers. This pattern exists in many other countries, but is particularly pronounced in Britain, partly resulting from tax and housing policy considerations. There is no particular reason why owner-occupation should be associated with wealth, or renting with lower income groups. It is not a case of owner-occupied housing being more expensive, because the same dwelling must cost exactly the same whether it is rented or owned, unless there is some distortion through the tax system or through restrictive legislation. Owner-occupation and renting are merely different ways of paying for the same commodity and they do not alter the basic price.

The very poorest people, in the third world countries, are unable to pay any rent because they have no income. They will, therefore, be classified as owner-occupiers even though they are inhabiting very basic accommodation. As incomes increase in developing countries so the proportion of the population renting can be expected to rise as some of those who can afford to rent a dwelling do so and hence transfer from owner-occupation.

In industrialized countries there is no reason to expect an exact correlation between wealth and housing tenure. If people can afford to buy or to rent, then the decision as to which tenure they have will depend on a number of factors of which income or wealth is not particularly significant. Probably the most important is whether the household intends to live in the dwelling for a long or short period of time. Owner-occupation inevitably carries with it substantial transaction costs, and, moreover, it generally takes a period of weeks, if not months, to complete the purchase of a dwelling. By contrast, rented housing, even though it may be more expensive, carries with it few transaction costs and can be acquired and disposed of very easily. In practice, it is often possible for a tenant to walk out of a dwelling with no loss to himself even if this is in breach of the tenancy agreement.

The general conclusion on this point must be that wealth is of direct importance in determining housing tenure only to the extent that people who have no income or wealth are not in a position to pay rent, and therefore are owner-occupiers of very poor property. Indeed, often they may be squatters. Beyond this there is no reason for any direct correlation between owner-occupation and wealth although there is a significant indirect correlation because of the age factor.

Age is a far more important direct variable. It is possible to devise a theoretical life cycle of housing requirements. In industrialized countries most new households are established by people between the ages of 20 and 25. The time at which a household is established will depend on a number of circumstances including real incomes, wealth and the availability of housing. The natural inclination of people at this age is to leave their parents' home to set up on their own, but the time when they are able to do so will depend on their income and the price and availability of housing. In recent years in all industrialized countries there has been a steady reduction in the age at which households are established, which largely reflects the increase in living standards.

Initially, most households will want to rent as this is the most flexible form of tenure. The point has been made that transaction costs are much lower than in the case of owning, and that a renting arrangement can usually be negotiated more quickly than the purchase of a house. When households first set up on their own they are not likely to want to remain in their first home for more than a short time. Their income at that stage will be comparatively low and they are unlikely to wish to commit themselves to a long-term housing arrangement based on a low level of income. Renting is therefore particularly suitable for young people who are anticipating only a short period of occupation, who may possibly wish to move between areas quite quickly, and who may also expect to set up household with another person fairly shortly when there would be different housing requirements.

It is at the stage when a household wants to settle roots more firmly, and that will often be on marriage, or on a permanent co-habitation arrangement, that owner-occupation becomes more attractive. Depending on circumstances, initially a small owner-occupied flat or house may be all that can be afforded, and subsequently larger units can be purchased as incomes increase and as there is a need to accommodate children. A decision between owner-occupation and renting will depend on a variety of factors, but generally the older a household the more likely it is to want to be more firmly settled, and hence the more attractive owner-occupation will be in relation to renting.

As households move into old age so the attractions of owner-occupation diminish. A house may be too large after children have left home and maintenance of it can become a burden, as the physical and sometimes financial capacity to undertake even basic maintenance and repair work diminishes. One would therefore expect moves into smaller owner-occupied units or into rented housing.

Generally, there are grounds for expecting a high level of renting among younger households and a very high level of owner-occupation in the middle and upper age groups with perhaps a slight tail-off in the older age groups. However, this theoretical pattern is capable of being greatly distorted by legislation on rented housing and by the operation of housing subsidies. These points will be illustrated more fully in the following section.

A final variable which influences housing tenure is physical location. One would expect owner-occupation to be higher in rural areas than in urban areas, reflecting the different characteristics of people who live in the two types of area. In rural areas the turnover of population is much lower and when people acquire housing it is likely to be for a fairly long time. Cities tend to attract younger and more mobile people and there is a more rapid turnover of population. A logical pattern to expect, therefore, is that owner-occupation is highest in rural areas and lowest in the centre of large cities.

This theoretical analysis of housing tenure leads to the following broad generalizations:

(1) The very poorest people in third world countries cannot afford to rent and therefore by definition are owner-occupiers but beyond this there is no necessary direct correlation between housing tenure and wealth.
(2) There are good grounds for expecting a life cycle of housing tenure with people initially being tenants then moving into owner-occupation and finally some moving back into renting.
(3) Owner-occupation is highest in rural areas and lowest in inner-city areas.

Patterns of Housing Tenure

The theoretical analysis is essential background to a consideration of patterns of housing tenure, and in this section the position in Britain is put into an international context.

Table 1.1 shows an international analysis of the proportion of owner-occupation in comparison with per capita income levels.

Table 1.1 *Per Capita Income Levels and Housing Tenure*

Country	*Owner-occupation %*	*Year*	*GNP per capita, 1981 (US$)*	*GNP per capita, 1980 (international $)*
Switzerland	30	1980	17,430	
Luxembourg	59	1981	15,910	10,630
Sweden	57	1981	14,870	
Norway	67	1980	14,060	11,330
West Germany	37	1978	13,450	10,200
Denmark	52	1980	13,120	9,830
USA	65	1981	12,820	11,450
France	47	1978	12,190	9,780
Belgium	61	1981	11,920	9,440
Netherlands	44	1981	11,790	9,320
Canada	62	1978	11,400	
Australia	70	1981	11,080	
Austria	50	1981	10,210	8,630
Japan	60	1978	10,080	8,410
United Kingdom	59	1981	9,110	8,250
New Zealand	71	1981	7,700	
Italy	59	1981	6,960	7,790
Spain	64	1970	5,640	6,350
Singapore	55	1980	5,240	
Eire	74	1981	5,230	5,488
Israel	71	1978	5,160	
Uruguay	52	1975	2,820	
Brazil	60	1970	2,220	
Hungary	76	1980	2,100	
Paraguay	82	1972	1,630	
Colombia	54	1973	1,380	
Philippines	89	1970	790	
Thailand	89	1976	700	
Pakistan	78	1980	350	
India	85	1971	260	
Bangladesh	90	1981	140	

Source: Boléat, 1985, p. 461 and OECD, 1985a, p. 13.
Note: Figures in final column show GNP per capita adjusted for differences in living costs and are a better indication of living standards than the figures in the previous column.

The theoretical pattern described earlier can be seen clearly. The very poor countries have extremely high levels of owner-occupation. In the industrialized countries it is very difficult to find a correlation between GNP per capita and the level of owner-occupation. Indeed, Switzerland stands out as having the highest GNP per capita and the lowest level of owner-occupation, and West Germany is another country with high incomes and low owner-occupation. Within Britain there is undoubtedly a correlation between income and owner-occupation. In the highest income groups over 80 per cent of people are owner-occupiers while in the lowest income group the proportion falls to 30 per cent. The reasons for this and other characteristics of housing tenure in Britain are discussed subsequently.

The theoretical life cycle of owner-occupation can be illustrated by the statistics for Great Britain, Canada and West Germany. These are shown in Table 1.2. It will be seen that each country has its lowest level of owner-occupation in the under 25 age group, with the peak figures occurring in middle age and, except in the case of West Germany, a slight decline in old age.

Table 1.2 *Owner-Occupation by Age, International Comparison, 1982*

Age of head of household	*Percentage of households*		
	Great Britain	*Canada*	*West Germany*
Under 25	30	17	4
25–29	54	44	15
30–44	67	68	53
45–59	59	78	
60–64	50	75	49
65+	45	61	63
Total	56	63	40

Source: BSA, 1985a, p. 10.

Table 1.2 provides a useful framework in which distortions to the theoretical pattern can be discussed. Especially in Britain, but also in many other countries, the theoretical life cycle of housing tenure does not correspond to reality because of legislation and regulations. In particular, there is not a free choice between owner-occupation and renting because of the distortions arising from the subsidy system and legislation controlling the level of rents. The figures for Britain show a very high level of owner-occupation among younger age groups compared with the two other countries, but a sharp decline in the older age groups. However, it needs to be noted here that this last phenomenon exists simply because people in the older age groups have never been owner-occupiers. Britain has been experiencing a very rapid growth in owner-occupation, probably unmatched in any other country, and as those in the middle age groups get older so the proportion of owner-occupation among the elderly will increase.

In Britain the subsidy system operates in such a way that the poorest people are better off as tenants, and middle and upper income people are better off as owner-occupiers. Moreover, the housing which is available to poor people is public authority rented housing, which for a variety of reasons which cannot be discussed here is unpopular. Such housing is also generally available only to families with children and to the elderly, and not to unmarried people or to young married couples without children. One therefore has a position that in Britain people want to be owner-occupiers at the earliest possible age and increasingly the only people remaining as tenants are those who find owner-occupation relatively expensive, given the subsidy system. This explains the extremely high level of owner-occupation amongst younger households in Britain. It probably does not reflect the true underlying demand, as many young households would prefer to rent for a few years before firmly settling their roots. Nevertheless, it is a factor which has to be taken account of in the housing finance system.

The contrast with West Germany is particularly marked. The normal pattern in that country is for people to rent perhaps three or four dwellings before they finally purchase their one and only owned dwelling, which they may well have built to order, when they are in their mid-30s. Such a dwelling will continue to be occupied into old age.

Table 1.2 provides powerful evidence on the effects of government regulation in overriding natural market forces. The figures for Canada, which has a housing system relatively undistorted by subsidies, are probably as near to a theoretically perfect pattern as one could expect. The figures for Britain reflect a housing system which allows little or no choice to many households but to become owner-occupiers and which provides rented housing only for the poorest people.

Finally, it is necessary to comment briefly on the differences in housing tenure by type of urban location. Table 1.1 provides useful information on this point. It may be noticed that of the English-speaking countries the Republic of Ireland and New Zealand have the highest levels of owner-occupation, at over 70 per cent. This is connected with the fact that of the English-speaking countries they are the most agricultural. More generally, the theoretical picture of there being a higher level of owner-occupation in rural areas is shown in countries at all stages of development.

For example, in the Philippines over 90 per cent of units in rural areas are owned whereas in urban areas the figure is little more than 60 per cent. In India in 1971, 74 per cent of units in rural areas were owned whereas in urban areas the figure was just 47 per cent. In France in 1975 the level of owner-occupation was 67 per cent in rural areas, 42 per cent in urban areas and only 34 per cent in Paris.

Comparable statistics for Britain are not available. Table 1.3 shows figures for West Germany which, although it has a low level of owner-occupation by international standards, has a fairly typical distribution by type of urban area.

Table 1.3 *Housing Tenure by Type of Location, West Germany, 1978*

Tenure	*Densely populated regions*		*Regions with small agglomerations*		*Rural areas*		*All areas*	
	000	*%*	*000*	*%*	*000*	*%*	*000*	*%*
Owned	4,107	30	2,744	46	1,671	51	8,522	37
Rented	9,698	70	3,198	54	1,588	49	14,484	63
Total	13,805	100	5,942	100	3,260	100	23,006	100

Source: Ministry of Regional Planning, Building and Urban Environment, 1982.

Thus patterns of housing tenure may be summarized as follows:

(1) The level of owner-occupation in Britain is not unusually high or low by international standards.
(2) Britain stands out from other countries in having a much higher level of owner-occupation among younger age groups, reflecting the lack of availability of rented housing.

House Purchase and Loan Finance

It might seem to be stating the obvious to say that in order to effect house purchase a loan is required. However, this is not necessarily the case. In third world countries most of the houses which are owner-occupied have been acquired or built without any loan finance, simply because the people concerned have no income to support repayments on a loan or because there are inadequate mechanisms to provide loan finance. Sometimes the houses have been built over a period of years as resources permit, and where external funding has been required this has been through informal loans from relatives or the sale of assets such as cattle and jewellery. As will be shown in Chapter 3, most developing countries have very small housing finance systems notwithstanding their high levels of owner-occupation.

In industrialized countries house purchase does require loan finance if the system is to operate efficiently. Housing yields a stream of services over a period of years and it is therefore logical that it should be paid for over a period of years by means of loan repayments rather than in one lump sum. If people had to pay for their housing in one go then very few would be able to afford housing until very late in life. Loan finance is therefore essential to make an owner-occupied housing market work with full efficiency.

The amount of loan finance needed by an individual will depend on a number of factors. An obvious one is the price of housing. This can differ from country to country for a number of reasons which cannot be considered in detail in this book. Obviously the higher the price of housing the greater the amount of loan finance that is required. This applies within countries as well as between countries. In order to buy a house in London, for example, a higher price has to be paid and therefore a larger loan is required compared with buying a house in another part of the country.

The age at which house purchase is effected is also important. The younger people are, the less opportunity they have had to build up savings. In Britain, where people purchase their first houses at a very young age compared with other countries, high percentage loans are required. In West Germany, where house purchase takes place much later on in life, lower percentage loans are required, but this is partly compensated for by the much higher house prices in West Germany. The funds required also depend on the stage the individual has reached in the cycle of house purchase. In Britain, although second buyers purchase a house that is, on average, twice as expensive as those purchased by people buying for the first time, the size of loan required by the two groups is roughly similar because the existing owner-occupier is able, and sometimes required, to use the capital gain on the first house to meet part of the cost of purchasing the second.

The proportion of people for whom it makes sense to purchase owner-occupied housing without loan finance is small, although by no means negligible. In England in the late 1970s, 17 per cent of those moving into, or within, the owner-occupied sector did not make use of a loan. Theoretically, one would expect those moving down market to be able to use the proceeds of the sale of their existing house to purchase another dwelling without recourse to borrowing. As noted earlier the elderly are likely to wish to move to smaller dwellings as their children leave home and maintenance of a family home becomes more difficult, and it is amongst the elderly that cash buyers are most likely to be found. Table 1.4 illustrates this.

Table 1.4 *Proportion of Movers in Owner-Occupied Sector Not Using Loans, England, 1977–8*

Age of head of household	*Total number moving (000's)*	*Percent not using loan finance*
Under 25	93	4
25–29	172	3
30–44	326	8
45–59	113	29
60 and over	81	79
All ages	784	17

Source: Office of Population Censuses and Surveys, 1983, p. 19.

The table and the previous paragraphs suggest that the overall size of the housing finance market could depend to some extent on the age structure of the population. However, as will be shown in the following chapter, the size of the market actually depends much more on a number of economic variables that are not wholly related to housing.

The Requirements of Housing Finance Systems

The housing finance market has different requirements from other financial markets because of the peculiar nature of the housing finance process. A particularly important requirement is the need for long-term finance. This is necessary because house prices are high in relation to incomes compared with other commodities. Unless loan repayments are spread over a long period they would be too high in relation to the borrower's capacity to repay. This is in contrast, for example, with loans to manufacturing industry which typically will have a shorter maturity reflecting the brief life of industrial equipment compared with housing. A house represents good security for a long-term loan, but this does not alter the difficulty of providing long-term finance.

Table 1.5 illustrates the need for long-term finance by showing monthly repayments on a £25,000 loan (the average new loan in 1985) for various mortgage rates and what those repayments would be as a percentage of income for someone earning £10,000 a year (the average male's gross earnings in 1985).

Table 1.5 *Mortgage Repayments for Different Mortgage Terms*

Mortgage term (years)	*Monthly repayments on £25,000 loan at 11% net of tax relief* £	*Percentage reduction on previous term*	*Percentage of gross earnings of person earning £10,000 a year*
5	519.75		62.4
10	308.50	40.6	37.0
15	241.25	21.8	30.0
20	210.00	13.0	25.2
25	192.75	8.2	23.1
30	182.50	5.3	21.9

The table shows that over five years the repayments would be impossibly high in relation to earnings and only with a ten-year term would they become reasonably manageable. Between twenty and twenty-five years the percentage reduction in payments is comparatively modest. The table itself is sufficient to show that house purchase loans ideally need a maturity of in excess of ten years and that even loans of fifteen or twenty years can lead to a significant reduction in monthly repayments in comparison with shorter terms.

A second characteristic of the housing finance market is that it must attract funds from outside the housing finance system. There may be attractions in constructing a scheme in which the savings of potential purchasers are used to fund mortgage loans, but in practice this is not possible. Even in countries such as West Germany where people buy houses fairly late in life, the accumulated savings of potential purchasers can never be sufficient to fund actual loans. In a country such as Britain where people buy houses at a very young age (a third of those buying for the first time are under the age of 25), purchasers may have held savings averaging perhaps £1,000 over three years and then expect a £30,000 loan to be repaid over twenty-five years.

The position can be illustrated by examining the life cycle of savings in the same way as the life cycle for housing has been examined. Young households have very small savings. Generally, their savings are short-term only, and used for specific purposes such as a new car, a holiday, household equipment and, of course, a house itself. Once the house has been acquired the household will be a substantial net debtor, although some liquid savings will be held for specific purposes. In middle and later age debts are gradually repaid, household income increases and the household is likely to become a net saver. It is also at this age that inheritances are most likely to be received and insurance policies mature. By the time they reach the 50s or 60s age group many households may have quite substantial savings.

Aggregate figures for some countries can illustrate this. In 1983, 59 per cent of the savings held in British building societies were held by those over the age of 55, and just 4 per cent by those under the age of 25; 83 per cent were held by owner-occupiers (BSA, 1983, p. 10). Similarly, in the USA in 1982, 48 per cent of savings balances held with financial institutions were held by those aged 65 or over, and only 1 per cent by those under the age of 25 (USLSI, 1983, Table 9).

A housing finance system therefore has to be able to attract savings from elderly people to lend to younger people, and potential borrowers are unable to provide any more than a small fraction of the total funds which the system requires.

A third requirement of housing finance systems is that they must have a delivery mechanism for making loans. Many of the largest financial institutions in the world deal largely with companies and governments and can operate through a small number of offices making very large loans. While loans for house purchase might seem high to individuals, they are very small in relation to many of the financial transactions carried out by banks. Often there is competition to obtain mortgage business and institutions seeking to provide loans have to attract that business. This can be done through offices in shopping centres, or it can be done through linking with other institutions in the housing market, in particular housebuilders and estate agents. Having made a loan, a housing finance institution also needs a mechanism for receiving the regular repayments and dealing with arrears problems. In the past this required a branch network, but with developments in technology this is no longer the case to the same extent.

In the USA in particular an industry has developed which has made the servicing of loans a function in its own right and it is now possible for institutions to provide mortgage loans without being bothered with the administrative problems of dealing with a large number of individuals.

A final special characteristic of housing finance loans is that ideally the borrower should be able to redeem them prematurely so as to make it possible to move house before the end of the loan term.

In some cases, of course, a loan can be taken over by the purchaser of a new house. This particular point shows the advantages of loans with variable rates of interest. Lenders can allow these to be redeemed without any risk of loss to themselves because they are always at market-related rates, and purchasers have no risk of being committed to a long-term fixed rate loan which might be substantially higher than market rates. Where an institution has made a long-term loan at a fixed rate it will generally have funded this by a long-term liability. If interest rates fall the borrower is likely to be dissatisfied and may even have difficulty in repaying his loan. If interest rates rise, the borrower is in an advantageous position. The relative merits of fixed and variable rate mortgages are discussed in Chapter 8.

2 Financial Intermediation and Housing Finance

Chapter 1 was concerned with real economic variables and commented briefly on their links with financial variables. In particular, the requirements of housing finance systems were indicated, but the point was made that economic and fiscal variables are likely to have as great an influence on the housing finance system as the more obvious housing variables. This chapter examines the concept of financial intermediation, types of intermediation and the factors affecting the size of housing finance markets.

The concept of financial intermediation is a very simple one. Intermediation occurs where an institution, such as a bank or building society, facilitates the transfer of financial resources from those individuals and institutions with surplus funds in relation to their requirements to those with a deficiency. Generally, the more sophisticated and less regulated the intermediation system, the smaller the gap between the rate paid to investors and that charged to borrowers.

An important measure of the efficiency of a system of financial intermediation is the ability to 'transform' funds. Writers on this subject usually talk about institutions' ability to undertake maturity transformation, risk transformation and geographic transformation. These three concepts are important in understanding the development of a housing finance system and are examined below.

As Chapter 1 explained, the expense of purchasing a dwelling is such that most individuals require long-term finance in order to complete the transaction. However, most individuals or organizations with surplus funds require at least part of those funds to be fairly readily available. One of the functions of institutions in the housing finance market is therefore to transform short-term savings into long-term loans. In the UK and 'old' Commonwealth countries short-term deposits are easily used to fund long-term mortgage loans through the use of the variable rate mortgage, which enables institutions to vary the rates of interest which they pay on their funds and charge on their loans simultaneously. This system is examined in detail in Chapters 4 and 8. In the mortgage banking system, examined in Chapter 5, institutional investors purchase long-term paper issued by housing finance institutions, generally at fixed rates of interest; the funds acquired are used to make long-term house purchase loans, generally also at fixed rates of interest. In this system providers of short-term funds are able to buy and sell the mortgage banks' debt, without affecting the long-term status of the mortgage loan. Liquidity, in this case, is provided by a secondary market in mortgage bank debt.

The second major function of a financial institution is to pool risks. An individual offering his entire savings to another individual wishing to purchase a house runs a considerable risk of losing those savings should the borrower default. A financial institution is able to spread the risk among thousands of depositors or bond holders and develop sophisticated systems for keeping risks of loss to a minimum.

Finally, a housing finance system must be able to transfer funds from those parts of the country which have a surplus to those parts which need to borrow. In the UK this type of transfer is undertaken within institutions. As most housing finance is undertaken by institutions operating on a national scale, funds raised in one part of the country can be lent in another part. In the USA financial institutions cannot easily operate outside their state of origin and a secondary market had to be developed to facilitate the movement of funds around the country. This subject is examined in Chapter 10.

The Financial Sectors of the Economy

To put the following discussion in perspective it is helpful to comment initially on the four financial sectors of an economy which are identified in national accounts. The four sectors between which funds can flow are the corporate sector, the public sector, the overseas sector and the personal sector. The flow of funds between these four sectors must, of course, balance, although in practice there are substantial residual items, notwithstanding the increasing sophistication of financial statistics.

In practice the government sector almost invariably (in the UK at least) has expenditure exceeding its income, which means that it has to be a net borrower from the other sectors. The overseas sector is the counterpart of the balance of payments. If there is a balance of payments deficit there must be an inflow of funds into the country which can be used to finance deficits in the other sectors. The corporate sector figure reflects profitability, cash flow and the need to finance new investment. The personal sector generally has a substantial surplus. The figures for the United Kingdom for 1985 illustrate the position. The corporate sector had a surplus of £7,400 million, the overseas sector had a deficit of £3,000 million and the public sector had a deficit of £10,300 million. The personal sector had a surplus of £10,500 million and there was a substantial balancing item of £4,600 million. The analysis is obviously far more complicated than this, not least because of the difficulty of measuring precisely financial flows within and between the sectors and even defining the sectors, but nevertheless this basic framework always holds good.

It should be noted that all the figures quoted are net. The fact that the public sector is generally in deficit does not mean that no funds flow from the government to the personal sector, because obviously they do. If one sector is in deficit this simply means that the flow of money from that sector more than outweighs the flow of funds into the sector. For example, in some countries, such as Norway and Sweden, the government provides loans for house purchase and there is therefore a gross flow of funds from the government sector to the personal sector, but this is probably outweighed by higher gross borrowing in the opposite direction leaving the government sector in deficit. In Britain there is now virtually no flow of government funds to the personal sector which is used to finance house purchase, although in recent years the personal sector has received large amounts of public sector grants to finance house improvement and repair. In no country does the corporate sector provide a significant amount of loans for house purchase and the overseas sector may be regarded as a residual in this respect. This means, in effect, that the personal sector is the source of funds for loans for house purchase. However, the personal sector is also the destination of those loans. There is therefore little point in looking at the net flow from the personal sector to the other sectors because this does not reflect housing finance activity except to the extent that the construction of new houses needs to be financed. This point is developed in detail in the following section.

Finally on this point, it may seem that in many countries loans for house purchase are provided by institutions which do not collect funds directly from the personal sector. Mortgage banks, which issue bonds on the financial markets, are one obvious example, and so to a lesser extent are insurance companies and pension funds. However, the fact that funds are not obtained directly from the personal sector does not mean that they do not ultimately come from this sector. An individual may deposit his savings in a bank, which in turn may buy the bonds of a mortgage bank, which in turn makes loans for house purchase. It is clear here that it is personal sector savings that are providing finance for mortgage loans albeit two stages removed. Again, this point is developed in detail below.

Financial Intermediation within the Personal Sector

The previous section has made the point that the aggregate flow of funds from the personal sector to the other sectors is of little relevance to the process of housing finance. This process, particularly in Britain, largely involves the interchange within the personal sector of real and financial assets and liabilities. The extent to which housing finance activity is entirely within the personal sector depends largely on the amount of finance which is used for the exchange of existing dwellings rather than the acquisition of new dwellings or repair and improvement work. In the latter two cases there is a flow of funds from the personal sector generally to the corporate sector, although much repair and improvement work, and a small amount of new housebuilding, is actually done within the personal sector.

More housing finance activity in Britain is within the personal sector than in other countries. Probably the main reason is that referred to in the first chapter: people become owner-occupiers very early on in life and this factor, together with the lack of available rented accommodation, means that there is a large turnover of houses. This is in contrast to West Germany where people tend to purchase one house only during their lifetimes. In Britain, as a result, most housing finance activity is in respect of existing rather than new dwellings. This is not true in some countries such as France and Germany where most lending is on new houses and so to a greater extent the housing finance system does involve funds raised in the personal sector being transferred to the corporate sector, although, of course, as those loans are gradually repaid so this diminishes.

The importance of intermediation within the personal sector can be illustrated by looking both at the individual and at the economy as a whole. An individual purchasing an existing house costing £30,000 with the help of a 100 per cent loan will repay that sum to a vendor who himself may use it to purchase another house. However, ultimately someone will receive money who is not purchasing another house, perhaps a person moving out of owner-occupation on retirement, or even the beneficiaries of an estate. The overall effect is that two parties have exchanged financial and real assets and liabilities with each other. It is possible that the vendor, on receiving the purchase price, places the money back with the building society or other lender which provided the loan to the purchaser. The overall effect on the rest of the economy if this occurs is zero, and there are no implications for the net flow of funds between the sectors. Similarly, an individual who has a £30,000 mortgage but also £30,000 of savings with a building society has net indebtedness of zero. If he uses his savings to repay his loan then his financial position is unchanged although the building society is £30,000 smaller. There is again no overall effect on the rest of the economy.

It is now necessary to look at the position from the point of view of the economy as a whole. This can best be done by using a modified sources and uses of funds table for the personal sector in the United Kingdom. Table 2.1 shows that saving, that is, personal disposable income less consumers' expenditure, totalled £27,770 million in 1985, which was less than half of the total funds available to the personal sector. Borrowing accounted for most of the remainder, with borrowing for house purchase alone accounting for more than £18,000 million. Capital transfers are of minor importance but include home improvement grants paid by the government to home owners. On the uses side, deposits with building societies were less than loans for house purchase, thereby indicating that the funds made available by building societies for house purchase exceeded the deposits placed with them, or in other words during the course of the year the personal sector increased its net indebtedness to building societies. The position can further be illustrated if it is assumed that building societies had decided autonomously to lend an additional £1,000 million in 1985. Only a small proportion of that amount could have gone into new housing and the rest could only have been absorbed in the second-hand market, which would have led to additional activity and additional receipts by vendors of just under £1,000 million, which in turn could have been invested back in building societies, deposited with other financial organizations (either in the form of saving or reduced borrowing), or spent.

Table 2.1 *Sources and Uses of Funds of the Personal Sector, United Kingdom, 1985*

Sources of funds	*£m*	*Uses of funds*	*£m*
Saving	27,770	Capital transfers	1,814
Capital transfers	2,307	Investment in fixed assets and stocks	17,774
Borrowing for house purchase	18,019	Acquisition of liquid assets	21,147
(of which building societies)	(14,234)	(of which building societies)	(12,938)
Other borrowing	8,134	Acquisition of public sector securities	654
Accruals and unidentified	3,369	Acquisition of life assurance and superannuation funds	17,739
		Acquisition of company securities etc.	471
Total	59,599	Total	59,599

Source: CSO, 1986a, Table 9.2.

The impact of housing finance activity on the real economy is considered below in Chapter 11. At this stage it is sufficient to note that in Britain, at least, the housing finance function largely reflects some individuals investing with building societies and others borrowing from them, the two roughly cancelling each other out. It would be possible for both of these figures to increase or decrease substantially without there being significant repercussions on the economy as a whole. For example, if it suddenly became less attractive to have mortgage debt then those people with both savings in building societies and loans from them might use the savings to repay the loans. Conversely, if the government suddenly made borrowing on mortgage much more financially attractive through a subsidy this could lead to an increase in borrowing from building societies and correspondingly also to an increase in investments with them or with other financial institutions.

The extreme lack of importance attributed to the level of saving in this analysis should be recognized here. The saving figure represents the difference between personal income and consumers' expenditure and shows the amount of funds available for investment in either financial assets or fixed assets. The gross acquisition of financial assets is not affected by the level of saving undertaken by the personal sector. Any level of gross acquisitions is consistent with any level of saving. Concern about the level of saving and the saving ratio (which is merely the ratio of saving to income) and its effect on the ability of building societies to attract deposits is therefore misplaced. The important factor affecting the size of the housing finance market is the level of imbalances within the personal sector, rather than its relationship as a whole to other sectors. As long as some people within the personal sector have surplus funds available for the acquisition of financial assets and others require funds in order to finance purchases there will be a demand for financial intermediation, and this is true whether the level of saving is zero, strongly negative or strongly positive. The next section of this chapter assesses the factors influencing the level of these imbalances within the personal sector.

Table 2.2 summarizes the statistics for the destination of building society loans in 1985. It is important to distinguish between net and gross figures for lending. The most relevant variable is net lending, which takes account of repayments of mortgage principal all of which must be in respect of existing dwellings already owned by the personal sector. The table shows that over 50 per cent of building society lending was on existing houses and this amount purely represented a transfer of funds within the personal sector. Over 40 per cent of lending was concerned with the real economy (i.e. with the use of real resources such as labour, bricks and wood), just less than half of which went to housebuilders, while the remaining 5 per cent represented sales of council houses.

Table 2.2 *Building Society Lending, 1985*

Destination of loans	*Gross*		*Net*	
	£m	%	*£m*	%
New houses (housebuilders)	2,872	11	2,872	20
Existing houses (personal sector)	19,434	74	7,532	53
Existing houses (public sector)	735	3	735	5
Other, largely repairs and improvements	3,180	12	3,180	22
Total	26,220	100	14,318	100

Source: BSA, 1986a, pp. 34–5.

The third row of the table refers to the special circumstances affecting the sale of council houses during the early 1980s in Britain. Essentially, this involved the exchange of real and financial resources between the personal and public sectors, rather than within the personal sector. However, this provides only a small caveat to the general principle that building society business facilitates the transfer of funds within the personal sector, rather than between the different sectors of the economy.

The Extent of Intermediation and the Size of Housing Finance Systems

Having explained the concept of financial intermediation it is now necessary to go on to consider why the extent of intermediation differs between countries and therefore why housing finance systems differ in size.

Logically, it might seem that given similar levels of owner-occupation and similar house prices in relation to incomes, then countries would have similar sized housing finance markets. That this is not the case is illustrated in Table 2.3, which shows very tentative estimates for identified house purchase finance in relation to GNP.

Table 2.3 *Identified House Purchase Finance in Relation to GNP*

Country	*Unit*	*Identified house purchase finance*	*GNP*	*Debt/ GNP*	*Proportion of owner-occupation*
Switzerland	SFbn	132	206	64	30 (1980)
USA	$bn	1,254	3,073	41	65 (1981)
West Germany	DMbn	595	1,599	37	37 (1978)
Canada	$bn	127	357	36	62 (1978)
UK	£bn	76	271	28	59 (1982)
Japan	Yen bn	40,355	263,939	15	60 (1978)
Italy	Lbn	26,775	465,790	6	59 (1981)
India	Rm	12,700			85 (1971)

Source: Boléat, 1985, p. 218, p. 392 and p. 461.
Note: Figures are all as at end 1982 except that for India which is as at end June 1981. The date for the owner-occupation statistics is shown in brackets.

The table needs to be interpreted with extreme caution. Differences in definition between countries mean that it does not strictly compare like with like; the figures for some countries probably include an element of finance which is not for house purchase while those for others exclude finance which cannot easily be identified as being for house purchase, but which is. Nevertheless, the table does usefully illustrate the lack of any clear correlation between the proportion of owner-occupation in a country and the size of the house purchase finance market.

One obvious conclusion from the table is that the size of the house purchase finance market depends to a very large extent on the sophistication of the financial system. Developing countries do not have well-developed financial systems and hence house purchase finance is very small compared with the position in industrialized countries. The figure for India illustrates this admirably. Within the industrialized countries Italy stands out as having a not very sophisticated financial system, especially in respect of house purchase finance, and in that country identified house purchase finance is very small when compared with a variable such as GNP. Switzerland is at the other extreme, in that it has a low level of owner-occupation, but seemingly a very large house purchase finance market. It is clear that financial sophistication alone is not sufficient to determine the size of house purchase finance markets.

A second important variable is the relative attractiveness of mortgage loans. To households with financial assets, whether or not they have a mortgage loan can be seen as an investment decision, as they have the alternative of liquidating some of their savings. The extent to which loans will be held in such circumstances will depend partly on the need to maintain some liquid assets but mostly on the net of tax rate of return on the loan when compared with the net tax rate of interest which can be obtained on investments. In countries where mortgage interest qualifies for tax relief it is often possible for an individual to obtain a higher net return on an investment than the net cost of his mortgage loan. This is particularly true where households pay tax at above the basic rate, because usually there are investment opportunities which enable them to pay no more than basic rate tax on their investments. For example, in Britain in June 1986 the mortgage rate, net of tax at the basic rate, was 7.81 per cent, and to an individual paying tax at the highest rate of 60 per cent the net of tax rate was 4.4 per cent. It was, at the same time, fairly easy for individuals to obtain a net of tax rate of 8 per cent or more on their savings if they were basic rate taxpayers, and even higher rate taxpayers could obtain yields of about this amount through purchasing tax free National Savings Certificates or low coupon government securities.

It follows that in countries where mortgages are relatively attractive to hold then the house purchase finance market is likely to be larger than in countries where mortgages are not so favourably treated. This factor is one of the most important is explaining why Switzerland has a high level of mortgage debt. The position was neatly summarized by Schuster and Beckstrom (1984, p. 19):

> Taxes must be paid on the 'opportunity' rent or value of owner-occupied homes. Government officials estimate the rental value of a home, and the homeowner must claim this rental value as personal income. The homeowner may, however, deduct his interest payments from his declarable income. Thus it is standard practice to take out a large mortgage, even if not essential for personal cash flow reasons, solely in order to offset

additional income tax which a homeowner must pay. This is particularly true for homeowners in the higher tax brackets.

The rate of inflation also influences the size of house purchase finance markets. When inflation was running at a very high level in many countries in the 1970s the real value of mortgage debt fell significantly. This was true both for the whole economy and also for the individual who is well aware that the higher the rate of inflation the more quickly his housing debt will fall in relation to income. This factor might help to explain why both Switzerland and West Germany have seemingly large housing finance markets in relation to owner-occupation.

A further important factor is the pattern of housing tenure. The analysis in Chapter 1 is relevant here. If people purchase houses at a very early age, as in Britain, then they will need much larger loans than if they purchase later on in life, as in West Germany. Also, if owner-occupiers move house more frequently then house purchase finance is likely to be greater as houses are continually refinanced at higher amounts to take account of inflation.

A final factor is the degree of government and trade regulation of the housing finance system. In Britain the authorities often exerted pressure on the main lenders, building societies, to keep the mortgage rate below a market clearing level, and this combined with the cartel arrangements operated within the industry to leave the housing finance market under-supplied, and therefore smaller than if market forces had been allowed to operate. Similarly, successive governments operated systems of monetary control that had the effect of preventing the banks from offering mortgage finance. In the USA usury laws in some states made mortgage lending unprofitable when market rates rose, leading to a reduction in the supply of finance.

It is clear from this analysis that housing finance systems cannot be analysed simply by reference to housing tenure. It is largely financial variables, in particular the sophistication of financial systems and the tax and other government regulations applying to housing finance, that dictate the size of a country's housing finance system.

Types of Housing Finance System: An Overview

Figure 2.1 shows in diagrammatic form the flows of funds between individual investors and individual borrowers by the various types of system.

The simplest way in which funds can be channelled from investors to borrowers is by direct lending. This is what frequently happens in developing countries. Those who need to acquire funds in order to pay for their housing borrow directly from individuals with surplus financial assets,

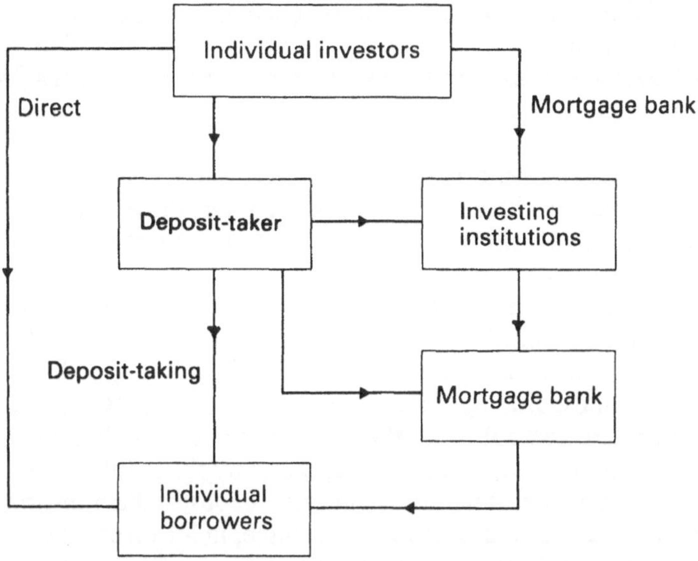

Figure 2.1 Types of Housing Finance System

often from within their family. The same happens to a limited extent in industrialized countries. It is not unusual for parents to contribute directly to the house purchase costs of their children and in some cases this may be through a loan, perhaps without interest.

In industrialized countries vendors may provide finance directly to investors, and this can be seen as another type of direct house purchase financing. The vendor obviously has available capital funds in the form of the housing which he wishes to sell and if he makes a loan to the purchaser he is in effect deferring the payment of part of the purchase price.

The one common characteristic of the various forms of direct financing is inefficiency. Transaction costs are likely to be high, bearing in mind that they are unlikely to be fully reflected in the price, if any, charged for the loan, and the chances of individual investors and individual borrowers having the same requirements with respect to the amount of the loan and its term are very low.

The simplest housing finance system which uses institutions is where individuals deposit funds directly with an institution and borrow from that same institution. The deposit-takers may be commercial banks, savings banks or specialist housing finance institutions such as building societies in Great Britain, Australia and South Africa, and savings associations in the USA. There is only one stage in this intermediation process; the public can clearly understand the relationship between the inflows of deposits and the amount of funds available, and the deposit-taking institutions can use marketing information gained from investors to help in their house purchase lending programme.

A slightly more complicated housing finance system involves a process of double or even triple intermediation. An institution which makes loans to individual borrowers is frequently called a mortgage bank; in some countries these are owned by governments. However, individual investors seldom place funds directly with a mortgage bank. Rather, these institutions obtain their funds through direct loans from deposit-taking institutions or through the sale of bonds which may be purchased by deposit-takers or investing institutions such as insurance companies or pension funds. Individuals do, of course, indirectly contribute to the funds of these institutions by making deposits in deposit-taking institutions and by contributing to life insurance and pension funds, although in countries such as Great Britain many such contributions are compulsory rather than made voluntarily by individuals. Where mortgage banks are state owned, they may obtain their funds through bond issues which investing institutions and deposit-taking institutions are required to purchase. This is true, for example, in Sweden. When mortgage banks operate within the private sector they may frequently be owned, partially if not wholly, by deposit-taking or investing institutions, and direct loans may be made from the parent institution to the mortgage bank. The parent institution, which is likely to have direct contact with individuals, can also introduce business to the mortgage bank. This system can be found in West Germany and Italy, and to a lesser extent in France also.

There are of course variations on these three types of system. For example, there is the closed system used in West Germany, France and Austria, whereby the savings of potential house purchasers are used partly to fund loans made to house buyers. This can be considered as a variant of the deposit-taking system. More importantly, a trend throughout the industrialized world has been for the barriers between financial institutions to break down. Specialist housing finance deposit-taking institutions such as building societies and savings associations have increasingly been raising funds from the wholesale markets, and more recently the international financial markets have also been used. The housing finance process has itself become fragmented, with some institutions originating and servicing loans which they do not hold, and in the United States in particular a thriving secondary market has developed, allowing mortgage loans to be directly financed from the capital markets.

Nevertheless the broad categorization of three types of housing finance system, together with the important variant of the contractual system, is still sufficient for analytical purposes and it will be used in Part II of this book.

PART II

Housing Finance Systems

3 Informal Housing Finance

This book is concerned primarily with institutional mechanisms for transforming personal savings into housing finance loans. However, to complete the analysis of house purchase finance it is necessary to consider briefly how house purchase is effected without institutional means. As a general observation it may be said that the institutional method of providing housing finance loans is efficient, and where institutions are not used this is either because they have not developed, as in the case of developing countries, or because they have been prevented from operating effectively, as sometimes occurs in industrialized countries.

Informal housing finance provides a useful test bed against which the institutional structure can be compared. If informal systems exist in industrialized countries this is an indication that something is wrong with the regulatory system. In developing countries evidence of a declining role for informal finance indicates the growing success of the institutions.

The Nature of Informal Finance

It is fairly easy to describe and explain the housing finance mechanisms of most industrialized countries. Statistics show the flow of savings from individuals to banks and other institutions, and the flow from there to home buyers. Where housing finance is conducted other than through institutions, then by definition there is a problem of description in that no statistics are available. It is in fact quite difficult even to explain fully what is meant by informal housing finance.

Perhaps it can be said that informal housing finance exists where a person buys or builds a house using finance other than a loan secured on the property at a rate of interest reflecting the nature of that security and market rates of interest, combined with a reasonable amount of personal savings (perhaps between 10 per cent and 30 per cent of the total cost). Informal finance can take several forms. At its simplest in developing countries it means that a person, instead of paying for a house to be built, builds it himself using 'sweat equity' and paying for materials as he can afford them. The process of construction may extend over ten or more years. Where finance is needed then among informal mechanisms are unregulated money lenders, loans from relatives, short-term bank loans, the forced sale of assets, credit provided by vendors, and, in the case of a person building his own house, credit provided by the supplier of materials.

The point has already been made that it is difficult to analyse informal housing finance because of its very nature. It cannot be analysed using published statistics, but rather analysis is dependent on surveys of particular markets at particular points of time.

Because the nature of informal finance is quite different in industrialized countries compared with developing countries they are considered separately in this chapter.

Informal Finance in Industrialized Countries

There will always be an element of informal finance in any housing finance system regardless of how sophisticated it is. It will exist because no market mechanism is perfect, and also because some people will in any event elect to use imperfect mechanisms because they are more familiar with them. Even in a country such as Britain, with a very sophisticated housing finance system, and even when it is working at its greatest efficiency, some young couples or single people will obtain part of the finance which they need to purchase their home through a loan from their parents. Where a gift is made this is in a quite separate category, which might also apply to an interest-free loan. If, however, the loan is supposed to carry a rate of interest that is approaching a market rate then this is clearly in substitution for using the institutional mechanism.

It is only in recent years that the demand for house purchase finance in Britain has been fully satisfied. Previously, building societies kept the mortgage rate below a market clearing level and this led to a significant element of informal finance. It included, for example, top-up loans from banks or insurance companies at much higher rates than the building society mortgage rate. In many cases it is probable that the average cost of the whole loan package was, because of the higher interest element, higher than what would have been a market rate of interest for mortgages. Mortgage rationing also meant that some people could not obtain building society loans at all and they may have resorted to a bank or other financial institution charging a much higher rate of interest for the whole loan. Where a loan smaller than the desired size was granted, obtaining funds from parents was an alternative to borrowing at a higher rate of interest from another institution.

Informal finance can often frustrate government policy in the housing market. A particular example of this occurred in 1978 when the government sought to control the rate of house price inflation by limiting the amount that building societies were able to lend. Societies reacted to this by turning away some potential borrowers and by reducing the amount lent to successful applicants. To the extent that this policy was effective, it was counteracted by increased reliance on the other sources of finance already described in this section. No attempt was made to limit parental help (probably in the realization that this would be impossible) and no controls were placed on other financial institutions. Individuals could therefore circumvent government policy by assembling their own loan packages, albeit at greater cost and at some inconvenience. The policy was soon seen to be unsuccessful and was discontinued.

Other countries have endured informal financing for long periods and in some countries it has been an almost permanent part of the system. Italy is a good example. Table 2.3 showed that identified house purchase finance in Italy is extremely low compared with other countries. The Italian financial system provides for a sharp division between banking institutions which are able to take deposits and long-term lenders which cannot. The main providers of mortgage loans are technically the special credit institutions, but they have seldom been able to meet demand. As a result banks have made available short-term loans which are continually being renewed and this can be seen as a type of informal housing finance. In fact bank lending for house purchase is much higher than lending by the special credit institutions, notwithstanding the fact that banks cannot normally make loans for longer than three years.

New Zealand provides another example. It has been the policy of the government to limit mortgage interest rates (although such limitations were removed in 1985). The government has also made available low interest loans through the Housing Corporation. The result has been a diversity of interest rates charged by lenders. In 1983, for example, 20 per cent of mortgage loans were made at a rate of interest of 10 per cent or under, and 34 per cent at a rate of 18 per cent or over.

In New Zealand borrowers have had to wait to obtain loans even from the private sector institutions such as building societies and savings banks, and this has led to a market in loans provided by solicitors for short terms, perhaps three years, at high rates of interest. Such loans continually require refinancing until a cheaper loan from one of the institutions becomes available. Generally, a two-year period of saving has been regarded as essential in order to secure a mortgage loan from a building society or a bank, and a deposit of at least 20 per cent is normally required. A first loan was unlikely to be sufficient to provide the remaining finance, with the result that second loans at higher rates of interest have also had to be obtained. Now that the government has removed interest rate controls it will be interesting to see how quickly the market responds.

The most common form of informal finance in industrialized countries is where the seller of the house provides the funds directly to the buyer. This can occur for new housing, where the housebuilder has to become a financial institution, and also for sales of second-hand dwellings where the vendor effectively defers payment of the purchase price for a time. In order to understand vendor financing it is necessary to examine several examples.

In developing countries it is fairly common for developers to provide loan finance because that is the only way that they can sell their houses.

Developers in turn have to obtain the necessary funds from the banking system and this can be regarded as a form of double intermediation. Even in a relatively industrialized country, such as Spain, many housebuilders still find it necessary to offer loan packages which they themselves have to fund. Naturally they are reluctant to do this because their expertise is in house-building, not in property finance, and capital tied up in long-term loans cannot be used to finance the building of more housing.

In Sweden in the 1970s what were called 'sellers' mortgage deeds' increased in importance as the mortgage credit institutes were unable, by regulation, to grant loans in connection with change of ownership. Rather, they were restricted to financing the purchase of new housing. However, in 1980 the institutes were granted permission to finance changes of owner-ship, as a result of which sellers' mortgage deeds lost much of their importance.

A more vivid example relates to the American experience in the late 1970s and early 1980s. The nature and extent of what has been called 'creative' financing has been described by Jaffee (1984) and Guttentag (1984). According to Jaffee's estimates, seller financing as a percentage of all mortgage originations of existing home loans rose from 2 per cent in 1977 to 50 per cent in 1981 before falling back.

The main cause of seller financing was a very sharp rise in market interest rates. At that time most loans in America were on the fixed rate basis. A borrower with a fixed rate of interest of, say, 5 per cent at a time when market interest rates were, say, 15 per cent naturally wanted to capitalize on his low interest rate loan. If he could sell the house with the loan still in force he could obtain a higher price than if a new loan had to be negotiated at the market rate of interest. However, institutional lenders were unwilling to provide the additional second mortgage financing required by the buyer and the value of the old mortgage could be realized only if the vendor provided the additional finance himself, which duly occurred. Here there was a definite gain to both lender and borrower, albeit at the expense of the financial institutions which were funding long-term fixed rate loans with short-term variable rate liabilities. Vendor loans were often provided at low interest rates and for short periods with no amortization, in the anticipation that they could be refinanced a few years later when interest rates fell.

A second factor leading to the emergence of creative financing was credit rationing by the institutional mortgage lenders, which, again, was caused by the sharp increase in market rates leading to a reduction in the flow of new savings to those financial institutions which specialized in making housing loans. The high rates also reduced the affordability of housing and some marginal borrowers were unable to obtain funds. Where, however, a vendor was anxious to sell he might be prepared in some cases to provide the loan finance himself, albeit at a risk of subsequent default.

This section has made it clear that the existence of informal finance in industrialized countries is a reflection of an inadequate institutional framework and, moreover, is largely, although not entirely, because of government regulation. Artificial controls on interest rates have led to informal financing in New Zealand. The Building Societies Association cartel, with government blessing, had the same effect in Britain, while restrictions on the ability of particular types of institution to lend for house purchase have had the same effect in Italy. The American experience was a consequence of a number of factors, including the institutions being forced to borrow short term at variable rates and lend long term at fixed rates. Over the past three or four years there has been a general recognition that market forces are more likely to lead to an equitable housing finance system, and controls on interest rates and on the composition of balance sheets have been dismantled. The result in Britain, and also in most other countries, has been that loans for house purchase have been more easily obtainable but at market rates of interest, as opposed to the previous position whereby some people had loans often at below market rates while others had to pay above market rates for their loan packages.

Informal Finance in Developing Countries

There are often only rudimentary financial systems in developing countries, and generally there is a correlation between the stage of development of a country and the level of financial sophistication in that country.

The very simplest forms of financial intermediation found in all developing countries are informal rotating credit societies and savings clubs. These exist under a variety of names but operate in a similar manner. The members contribute a set amount each week or month and each member of the society has a right to the funds under a procedure which is laid down. In some cases lots are drawn to decide who has access to the funds in which case no interest is charged. This is similar in concept to the old terminating building societies in Britain which allocated loans by balloting members. In other countries interest is charged and access to funds is determined by bids rather than by drawing lots.

The main retail financial institution in the poorest countries is often a government-owned post office savings bank system, generally without a lending function. This is true in Pakistan and Bangladesh, for example. In the more developed third world countries savings banks independent of post offices also exist, and in some countries commercial banks have a role in collecting retail savings. Often the savings banks have no lending function but rather pass over all of their funds to the government.

The stage of development of financial systems in developing countries is such that most housing investment is financed other than by institutional means. Generally, under 20 per cent of housing investment is financed by the formal sector and in some countries the proportion is under 10 per cent.

It is the nature of housing finance, together with the relative lack of sophistication of financial systems, which explains this phenomenon. Housing finance represents particular difficulties in developing countries. It involves dealing with households rather than companies and many households are unaccustomed to dealing with financial institutions and with concepts such as interest and repayments. Financial institutions have often found it unprofitable to deal with households because of the high transaction costs involved.

The point has already been made that ideally a house purchase finance system requires long-term loans, and again this presents particular problems in developing countries. The task is even more difficult where there are high rates of inflation; in some Latin American countries inflation rates have been well in excess of 100 per cent a year and in some cases, for example Argentina and Bolivia, well over a 1,000 per cent a year. Even inflation rates of 20 per cent or 30 per cent a year, which have been recorded in many developing countries, present acute problems for housing finance systems. Indexation has proved to be one answer, although not fully effective, in some Latin American countries, but in others this would not be a practicable proposition.

It is difficult to describe in detail how the informal system works, but there are some common themes. The first point which needs to be noted is that most house construction is actually carried out by the informal sector, often meaning the household, so it is not a question of informal financing being used to purchase houses built by registered housebuilders. Both the housing and the housing finance are conducted on an informal and indeed illegal basis.

The first stage of the process is the acquisition of land. In many cases this means squatting or the illegal sub-division of plots. Where a payment is made, as in the case of a sub-division, then this would be made through instalments. Where capital is used to finance construction then the main source is invariably personal saving. In some countries the government social security system can be used as security for funds or even to provide funds directly. For example, in Colombia, every employer must by law pay *cesantias* or severence pay to each employee on termination of employment, and this can be used to obtain advances from the employer for purposes related to housing. Blaesser (1981) has shown that it is the second major source of capital after savings. In developing countries generally construction is normally undertaken by the head of the household assisted by members of the family. It can often be a long-term process extending over ten or more years. As rooms are completed they may be rented out to help provide the income needed to pay any debts. Where materials are bought then the supplier will often provide credit which again is generally repaid out of income. Where funds need to be borrowed and cannot be obtained from relatives they are likely to be obtained from informal bankers which operate in many communities.

In the section on industrialized countries the point was made that informal housing finance systems cannot be efficient and that in the case of industrialized countries they reflect imperfections within the market generally caused by government actions. In the case of developing countries informal systems exist because of the lack of sophistication of financial systems, but in some cases government action has also played a part. There is a lively debate among housing finance experts as to whether the right policy prescription is to try to drive out the informal sector by making it illegal or rather whether its role should be specifically recognized and attempts made to link it with the formal sector, and in the longer term for formal sector institutions to develop in such a way that they drive out the informal ones because they are more efficient.

Certainly informal methods have to be recognized, not least because they finance over 80 per cent of housing investment. The informal sector is successful because it conforms to the appropriate market conditions. It is based on the family or the group towards which people in developing countries can feel some affinity, whereas they can feel no affinity for financial institutions. Loan recovery is a particularly difficult problem for formal institutions but in informal communities pressure can be put on a borrower through the community. However, informal systems must remain inefficient. Inadequate sums are raised which is why construction has to be phased over a longer period of time. Long-term loans are almost impossible and the costs of intermediation are very high, although probably no higher than those which are initially incurred by formal institutions. Informal systems also tend to be too small to be efficiently managed, typically involving no more than 100 people.

As financial sophistication increases, and given appropriate government policies, the role played by formal financial institutions can also increase. Formal institutions are, however, more likely to develop where there is economic stability. In countries where there is a high level of inflation people are more likely to hold their savings in relatively unproductive forms, such as jewellery and cattle, rather than financial assets.

In many countries interest rate controls have been imposed, ostensibly to protect borrowers. Invariably the effect has been to discourage the operation of the formal institutions and to encourage a black market for loans. However, it is increasingly being recognized that if formal institutions are to expand, then they must be allowed to operate at market rates of interest. Also, they must be allowed to make loans rather than simply hand over all their funds to the government. Where people in a community can see that the institution makes loans to that community, they will be more willing to invest with it than if they believe that the money is being handed over to the government, which may well not use it efficiently.

The formal institutions themselves can take steps to increase their role in the provision of housing finance. Contractual savings schemes, while they may provide only limited funds, can help to establish a direct link between saving and borrowing. The establishment of branch networks can bring an institution much closer to local communities although there is a danger of over-stretching resources. Savings schemes can be developed with individual companies and links established with informal institutions. However, having made these points it is clear from an examination of housing finance institutions in developing countries that most raise their funds predominantly from wholesale markets simply because the retail market is not sufficiently large. In terms of the analysis in this book, therefore, the formal institutions in developing countries tend to operate on the mortgage bank principle, but most housing finance is conducted through informal means, in other words the direct system. Ideally, in the longer term, the deposit-taking system must gain ground at the expense of both the other types, and this is often the objective of the authorities.

A Case Study: Housing Finance in India

India is a suitable country for a very brief case study on informal housing finance, largely because it is well documented. India is one of the poorest countries in the world with a level of income per head which is well below that of most of the other Asian countries, such as Thailand and the Philippines. In 1981 it is estimated that there were more than 20 million more households than serviceable housing units and much of the housing that does exist is very poor quality. Investment in housing is also exceptionally low and the public sector plays a very small part here, although this is not untypical.

The operation of the informal system is well illustrated in a study, albeit based on a small sample, of new housing in two Indian towns. Table 3.1 shows how savings provided most of the finance for new housebuilding. The second major source was the sale of assets, which may be regarded as transforming one type of saving into another. As noted earlier, assets here are likely to include jewellery and cattle. The institutions making long-term loans accounted for a very small proportion of funds and where bank loans exist these are likely to be short-term rather than long-term housing loans. The figure for 'other loans' is thought to represent loans from informal bankers or money lenders.

These figures alone are sufficient to show the very small role played by formal financial institutions. The most important formal institution has been the Life Insurance Company of India (LIC) which is nationalized, and the lending of which is subject to state control. Housing accounts for about 11 per cent of its total lending. It does not lend directly to house buyers but rather lends to state governments and to co-operative societies, various

Table 3.1 *Sources of Finance for New Houses, India, 1981*

Source	*Surat (152 units)* %	*Villupuram (47 units)* %
Savings	67	53
Sale of assets	6	14
Loan from provident fund	1	0
Loan from employer	1	0
Loan from Life Insurance Company (LIC)	2	0
Loan from Housing Development Finance Corporation (HDFC)	2	0
Loan from banks	9	4
Loan from relatives	8	5
Other loans	5	24
Total	100	100

Source: Lall, 1982, p. 74.

housing boards and another public sector body, the Housing and Urban Development Corporation (HUDCO). A significant role in housing finance is played by Apex Co-operative Societies. There are eighteen state-level societies and some 30,000 primary societies which obtain their funds largely from the state-level societies, but also from central and state governments. The primary societies, which have over 15 million members, actually build houses for their members. The LIC is a primary source of finance for the system.

The Housing and Urban Development Corporation was established in 1970 and like LIC does not lend directly to individuals but rather makes loans to others, in particular state housing boards. It obtains its funds from long-term borrowing, including from LIC.

The most interesting housing finance organization in India is the Housing Development Finance Corporation (HDFC). This institution was set up by an Indian development bank, the Industrial Credit and Investment Corporation of India, the International Finance Corporation and the Aga Khan, which between them provided 15 per cent of its share capital. The remaining share capital was obtained from a public offering. HDFC has subsequently grown rapidly into a significant mortgage bank. It obtains its funds through long-term lines of credit and special deposit schemes, rather than through personal savings. However, it is gradually evolving into a thrift institution, although it recognizes that this will take time.

On the lending side HDFC mainly finances individuals, but it also makes loans to companies to finance housing construction for employees, and it provides finance, through employing institutions, for their employees' individual homes. HDFC has been particularly successful in expanding lending to the lower income groups, and over half of its loans are to households earning less than the Indian equivalent of $250 a month. HDFC has been assisted by loans and technical assistance from the United States Agency for International Development. Table 3.2 shows the most recent balance sheet for HDFC.

Table 3.2 *Housing Development Finance Corporation, India, Assets and Liabilities, June 1985*

Liabilities	*Million rupees*	%	*Assets*	*Million rupees*	%
Loans			Housing loans		
From banks	281	9	Individuals	1,942	63
Under USAID programme	300	10	Corporate bodies and co-operatives	387	13
			Other	18	–
Army Group Insurance Fund	150	3	Investments	172	6
			Net current assets	512	17
Life Insurance Co. of India	100	3	Fixed assets	18	–
Other loans	50	2	Other assets	16	–
Bonds	200	7			
Certificates of deposit	1,764	58			
Loan linked deposits	12	–			
Share capital	100	3			
Reserves and surplus	108	3			
Total	3,065	100	Total	3,065	100

Source: HDFC, 1985.

HDFC executives have delivered many papers on housing finance and have become a principal source of information on the development of housing finance in third world countries. They have been instrumental in changing government policy in a number of areas, and have pointed to the need for various reforms. One of the problems at present is that there is not an effective foreclosure system, and generally in developing countries the adequacy of proper title systems is a major constraint on the development of both housing and housing finance. (It should be noted that this can also be a problem in some industrialized countries. In the USA, for example, there is no proper system of land registration and a large title insurance industry has developed.) People are reluctant to invest in housing unless they can be certain of their entitlement to the land and lending institutions are much better able to lend at reasonable rates of interest where they have adequate security and adequate remedies in the event of mortgage default.

Some of the problems which housing finance institutions in developing countries have to face in obtaining repayment of loans were illustrated in a paper by Shah (1984):

> Coming to lending, one of the problems that HDFC has encountered is in assessing incomes of the applicants. Self-employed individuals with small incomes are not required to pay income-tax and so there is no possibility of verification of income from their tax returns. HDFC has resorted to innovative techniques for this purpose. For instance, while lending to a cooperative society of small traders in a small town in Gujarat, our credit officer had to spend hours with vegetable vendors and small grocers at their stalls by the roadside to estimate their incomes. HDFC has occasionally found that such people do not even have bank accounts; they have then to be encouraged to open a bank account and deposit a small sum every month in those accounts to enable them to service our loan conveniently.
>
> Many of these borrowers are not literate and are not even in a position to fill up an application form for a loan. The problem is further compounded because there is no uniform language for communication.
>
> HDFC has to help out individuals in deciding on the loan amount to be applied for, as well as in filling up the forms. More importantly, individuals have sometimes to be educated about the obligation to repay the loan in a timely fashion. In the past, there have been various occasions when government and government agencies have provided loans, especially in small towns and rural areas, which have then been written off resulting in individuals developing the belief that loans need not be repaid.
>
> An interesting problem that HDFC has encountered concerns collection mechanisms in respect of borrowers whose income arises irregularly, as in certain self employed cases, or on daily basis, as in case of workmen. For instance, HDFC has provided loans on a pilot basis for a housing project in a tribal area of Valod. The loans range from Rs 1,000 ($100) to Rs 3,000 ($300) per dwelling unit and the cost of the dwelling units is a maximum of Rs 5,000 ($500); the borrowers include agricultural labourers earning about Rs 10–12 per day during the sowing and harvesting seasons and possibly nothing for part of the year. HDFC, along with a local voluntary agency in that area, is encouraging these individuals to save on a daily basis out of their income to facilitate repayment of the loan. HDFC is also discussing with agencies the possibility of setting up a service agency in each village which would be responsible for collection of the loans for a small fee.
>
> All these factors greatly increase the cost of servicing loans to low income individuals. Coupled with this is the fact that the loan amount is small. Therefore, the profitability of loans to low income individuals is not

very attractive. In case of arrears in repayment of such loans due to illness or loss of employment, the lending agency would have little choice but to reschedule such loans. Fortunately, HDFC has not had occasion to reschedule any loan, but the possibility always exists.

HDFC recognizes that it has only begun to scratch the surface and as yet it still accounts for a very small proportion of housing finance in India. In terms of total assets it is no larger than the thirtieth largest building society in Great Britain, in spite of its spectacular rate of growth. However, it provides a valuable demonstration of what can be achieved, and much of the success of HDFC is in spreading knowledge and thereby acting as a catalyst for the development of more effective housing finance systems generally. It is particularly significant that HDFC has had to operate as a mortgage bank despite its obvious preference to obtain retail deposits. It has used its lending to encourage deposit-taking, and over the years hopes to develop into a savings institution.

4 The Deposit-Taking System

The deposit-taking system is the simplest institutional mechanism for providing housing finance. People make deposits with deposit-taking institutions which lend those funds back to individuals who wish to borrow to buy a house. In some countries deposit-taking institutions concentrating on housing finance have tended to operate on different circuits from other financial institutions, but increasingly the various financial markets have been integrated and housing finance institutions relying on deposits have been forced into offering a wider range of financial services. The ability to specialize is declining.

Theoretical Issues

The deposit-taking system of housing finance is relatively easy to explain. In any advanced country there are institutions such as savings banks and commercial banks which collect retail deposits. These institutions therefore have funds available which they can use, in part, to fund house purchase loans. Maturity transformation is generally necessary because most deposits are short term (as depositors wish to have easy access to their funds), whereas housing finance loans have to be long term. Deposit-taking institutions therefore mobilize a large number of small deposits on a short-term basis and transform them into a smaller number of long-term loans to finance house purchase. The system has some attractions to the individual because there is only one organization involved and it is readily apparent that the institution with which he may make deposits is also that which he can approach for a loan. The direct connection between the saving and lending functions and the rates of interest on savings and loans can be seen. Moreover, deposit-taking institutions tend to have High Street outlets, and are therefore familiar to their customers and potential customers.

Deposit-taking institutions can raise their funds from the personal sector, from the corporate sector, or from other financial institutions. Corporate sector deposits are likely to be relatively stable and reflect the need of institutions to hold cash balances sufficient for running their business, but generally no more. Nevertheless, the total amount of corporate deposits held can be quite large.

Deposits from other financial institutions have been playing an increasingly important role in the financial markets. Banks make loans to each other through instruments such as certificates of deposit, and the wholesale money markets now provide an important source of funds to deposit-taking institutions in many countries.

However, it is the retail deposit-taking function that is of most interest in the context of housing finance loans. There are two reasons for this. The first is that in Britain, and many other countries, the institutions which make housing finance loans raise almost all of their funds from retail deposits rather than from the wholesale money markets. The second reason is that retail deposits increase over time, as financial wealth increases, and also as countries become more sophisticated financially. Chapter 3 showed how in developing countries economic development generally coincides with an increase in financial intermediation, and even in industrialized countries there are always some people who make only limited use of financial institutions, instead preferring to keep what savings they have in cash; more such people could be brought into the deposit-taking system.

One can also add an important third reason, which is that in countries such as Britain, where much housing finance activity is in respect of the second-hand market, the loans made by housing finance institutions can very quickly turn into deposits with those same institutions, or with other deposit-taking institutions, as explained in Chapter 2.

The retail deposits which institutions can attract can be divided into two main categories. The first, and often thought to be the most important if not the only source, is saving out of income. For an individual this is equal to the excess of his income over his expenditure and, similarly, for the personal sector as a whole saving is equal to the excess of personal disposable income over consumers' expenditure. In the national accounts the figure for saving is before acquisition of capital assets, whereas most individuals do not regard the acquisition of their largest capital asset, their house, as saving but rather as spending. Nevertheless, the same concepts apply for both the individual and the economy as a whole.

The volume of saving out of income is inevitably fairly limited. Most households do not have huge excesses of income over expenditure. Indeed, many households have an excess of expenditure over income. A typical household might perhaps generate modest net saving in its early years until such time as house purchase is effected, but for the next ten, twenty or even thirty years many households will then have very little net saving out of income. Certainly, there will be short-term savings and, indeed, a seasonal pattern can be discerned from disaggregated figures for building society inflows. Savings tend to be quite high in the early months of the year. They then fall off sharply in May and June, the peak months for payments for holidays, rise slightly in July, fall heavily in August, which is the month when most new cars are purchased, and rise strongly in the autumn, and then fall in December because of Christmas expenditure. Within the seasonal pattern individual households will also have a cyclical pattern of saving for large items of expenditure such as motor cars, home improvements and so on. Thus much saving out of income is short term and often with a specific objective in mind, although the total balances held in this way can be very substantial.

Where individuals have a permanent excess of income over expenditure, deposit-taking institutions may be used as a warehouse for savings until such time as they can be invested in a more profitable outlet. The people with the highest amount of saving will often be higher rate tax payers who in Britain can generally obtain a better net of tax return from various government instruments or who will wish to invest in instruments offering the prospect of a capital gain, which are taxed more lightly than interest payments.

The second source of deposits from the retail sector is capital sums. These tend to be received by people later on in life and could derive from a number of sources. Perhaps the most important one, and, given the rising level of owner-occupation amongst the elderly, one that is likely to become increasingly important, is inheritances from parents, and, to a lesser extent, other relatives. Most people die between the ages of 60 and 80 and it follows that money (often resulting from the sale of the family home) will be inherited by their children probably between the ages of 40 and 60. This is a time when most families have little need of additional capital, and the funds so received typically might be partly spent on a major purchase, such as a motor car, but much of it will be saved.

A second important source of capital sums is maturing life insurance policies. Many households take out such policies and will seek a maturity near their retirement so they have adequate capital funds off which to live in retirement. Again, such sums are typically received between the ages of 50 and 60. Lump sum payments on retirement are similar and are also likely to be received by the same age group.

Thirdly, and probably less importantly, redundancy payments can be important in some economies at certain stages of their economic cycle. Unemployment rose strongly in Great Britain in the early 1980s and some groups were compensated for the loss of their jobs by lump sum payments.

Finally, there are the proceeds of house sales. On moving house many households will show a profit which often will be ploughed into the new dwelling. However, in some cases it will suit a household not to reinvest all of the proceeds in the new house, but rather to hold some in liquid form. Moreover, when some households reach old age they may well deliberately trade down market with a view to freeing equity so as to provide capital on which income can be earned.

Capital sums are therefore an extremely important source of funds for deposit-taking institutions. The ability of an institution to attract such funds is likely to depend on the relative attractiveness of the rates of interest it is offering as against those offered by competing institutions and the tax regulations relating to the payment of such interest.

The different behaviour of saving out of income and the receipt of capital sums is illustrated in Table 4.1, which shows the net inflow of funds into building societies by size of transaction. Net receipts of small sums up to £500 may be regarded as saving out of income, and the seasonal pattern is evident with low points in December and the summer months, and high points in October, January and February. The figures for £500 to £2,000 are often low and sometimes negative. This reflects a typical pattern of relatively small deposits being accumulated and a large withdrawal being made to fund a major item of expenditure, for example, a motor car or investment in a different type of financial asset such as equities (the figures for November 1984 are affected by the British Telecom flotation), or an attractive issue of National Savings Certificates (such as in August 1984). The figures show that the major source of funds is net receipts in excess of £2,000, and in a number of months net receipts in excess of £10,000 have accounted for more than half of the total. Clearly these figures represent capital receipts and not saving out of income.

Table 4.1 *Net Receipts by Building Societies by Size of Transaction, 1984–5*

Month	*Net receipts (£million)*				
	Up to £500	*£501-£2,000*	*£2,001-£10,000*	*Over £10,000*	*Total*
1984					
January	300	90	192	349	931
February	286	106	203	363	958
March	272	76	94	291	733
April	122	64	178	322	686
May	83	–23	82	343	485
June	109	66	157	303	635
July	102	78	119	314	613
August	57	–4	–177	258	134
September	187	87	171	446	891
October	274	175	235	446	1,130
November	0	–33	31	367	365
December	43	277	242	449	1,011
1985					
January	320	127	75	301	823
February	313	96	–58	123	474
March	251	64	–151	50	214
April	149	63	8	287	507
May	47	49	82	437	615
June	3	46	–6	358	401
July	–14	29	36	599	650
August	–32	19	–23	560	524
September	73	37	19	468	597
October	194	134	17	451	796
November	30	101	77	430	638
December	–73	233	198	507	865

Source: BSA (unpublished).

The deposit-taking system of providing housing finance loans has a number of inherent advantages and disadvantages. The point has already been made that for the individual the system has the advantage of using familiar institutions. For the institutions themselves this is also advantageous; they have High Street outlets with which they can attract business and to some extent service loans. Also, where a potential mortgage applicant has had another financial account with an institution, that institution is better placed to make a credit assessment; a savings record is particularly important here.

However, the system also has its disadvantages. In particular, the process involves attracting a large number of small and fairly volatile deposits and this is costly, both in terms of branch networks and also handling the regular and usually increasing flow of payments into and out of accounts. Moreover, the deposit-taking system can raise only short-term funds. These can be transformed into long-term loans, in particular by using variable rate instruments, but it is also unlikely that the short-term retail deposit market is sufficiently large to attract all of the funds needed to meet the demand for house purchase finance at what is regarded by borrowers as a reasonable rate of interest. In many countries the deposit-taking system has been accompanied by an almost permanent shortage of mortgage finance, and topping up from longer-term sources has been necessary.

To the student of banking the deposit-taking system might seem to break the cardinal law of banking, that is, that one should not borrow short and lend long. At first sight it does seem strange that institutions can raise deposits almost all of which can be withdrawn at little or no notice, and lend them for twenty-five years. Borrowing short and lending long is dangerous because of the potential mismatch of assets and liabilities. However, this applies only if the lending is at fixed rates of interest. Clearly, an institution raising deposits at, say, 9 per cent and lending for twenty-five years at a fixed rate of, say, 10 per cent is very vulnerable if the cost of its deposits rises above 10 per cent. Where, however, the rate of interest on loans can be changed at little or no notice then effectively the institution is not borrowing short and lending long at all because its assets are effectively short term. Thus the deposit-taking system, in an environment of unstable interest rates, almost certainly requires variable rate mortgages and these have been normal in the United Kingdom, Australia and South Africa. However, this has not been the case in the USA and as a result the institutions which made long-term fixed rate housing loans were put in severe financial difficulty in the late 1970s and early 1980s when short-term interest rates rose rapidly. The question of the variable rate mortgage is examined in detail in Chapter 8.

Until fairly recently it was possible for institutions using the deposit-taking system to operate on fairly separate financial circuits from other institutions. They could offer just a good rate of interest without money transmission facilities, and often commercial banks and other potential mortgage lenders were not active in either the mortgage market or the retail savings market. This situation has changed over the past few years. The market for retail financial services has become increasingly competitive and modern technology makes it relatively easy to provide a basic money transmission service together with market rates of interest, a point examined more fully in the following section.

Raising Retail Funds

Traditionally, retail banking has been associated with branch banking. Retail deposits are attracted over the counter in High Street locations. Branches are particularly important for generating new business and often a customer will open his first account in the nearest branch to his home or place of work, and may then continue to use that institution even if others are capable of offering him a better service. In Britain, in particular, accounts are often opened by and for children, increasingly at a very early age. Branches are important here because no other method of paying money into or out of accounts is likely to be acceptable to children.

Until recently branches were very convenient for individuals to obtain cash when they needed it and for making deposits. Thus many people were paid in cash and would visit the building society as soon as they had been paid to make a deposit, and when they needed to withdraw a large cash sum, or simply needed additional cash for their day-to-day requirements, they could also visit a building society to make a withdrawal. As salaries have increasingly been paid by cheque and credit transfer so the money coming into building societies, and also money being paid out, has increasingly been other than in cash. Now, many building societies allow salaries to be paid directly into accounts, perhaps with a monthly payment to a bank account to provide the necessary finance to meet cheque payments.

The previous section of this chapter noted that most of the funds which building societies in Britain raise are capital sums rather than regular savings out of income, and here branch networks play a different role. Such money is often directed into building societies by intermediaries such as solicitors, estate agents and accountants. Inheritances, for example, may be paid through a solicitor and he may well offer to invest the money in a suitable building society. The proceeds from a house sale may be channelled by an estate agent into a building society. Branches are still important for this business because a manager has to establish contact with local professional people so as to persuade them to invest their funds in his particular building society.

Finally, deposit-taking institutions can raise funds by post. Once accounts have been established money can be paid into them, and to some extent paid out, by post and also new investors can be attracted by newspaper advertising. There are a few building societies in Britain which have concentrated on raising funds by this means rather than by establishing branch networks. This probably requires a higher rate of interest to be paid than for over the counter savings but on the other hand management expenses are considerably reduced.

It is now necessary to consider in more detail the rapidly changing nature of the market for personal financial services, and how this affects deposit-taking institutions. The various trends are illustrated in the following section which looks at specific types of deposit-taking institutions.

Specialist Housing Finance Deposit-Takers: Building Societies

Largely for historical reasons, in a number of countries, particularly English-speaking countries, a group of institutions have developed which raise deposits and use those funds primarily to make house purchase loans, and which account for a significant proportion of the market. These institutions originated in Britain and were exported from Britain to other English-speaking countries. Indeed, they are almost unknown in other parts of the world. In brief:

(1) In Britain building societies account for 75 per cent of the mortgage market and raise almost all of their funds through retail deposits.
(2) In Australia building societies are very similar to their British counterparts but account for only 40 per cent of the housing finance market.
(3) In South Africa the building societies account for some 70 per cent of house purchase finance.
(4) In New Zealand the building societies have only a small share of the mortgage market, about 20 per cent.
(5) In the USA institutions originally founded as building and loan associations have gradually changed their names to the more appropriate savings and loan associations, and more recently to savings associations and then to federal savings banks. Until about 1980 they were similar in concept to British building societies, raising their funds through short-term deposits and accounting for about 50 per cent of the housing finance market.
(6) Canada stands out against the general trend with no specialist housing finance institutions, although trust companies have certain similarities in that their liabilities are dominated by retail deposits and their assets by mortgage loans, but they have traditionally provided a much wider range of financial services.

It is the British building societies which best illustrate both the traditional specialist housing finance deposit-taker, and also how the role of specialist institutions is changing. The first building societies were founded in the late eighteenth century and as their names suggest they were societies comprising perhaps no more than twenty men who pooled their funds together to build themselves houses. During the nineteenth century societies gradually evolved from mutual building clubs into permanent housing finance institutions. A comprehensive Act in 1874 set out the legal framework under which societies have since continued to operate. In the first eighty years of the twentieth century, building societies changed comparatively little except in the size of their operations. A succession of Acts limited their powers strictly to raising retail savings and lending on mortgage, but the industry grew very rapidly and was characterized by increasing concentration reflecting the mobility of the population. The early societies had all been small local institutions but as communications improved so branch networks were increasingly established and a few societies, by the early 1950s, had become truly national institutions.

Building societies were undoubtedly assisted in their activities by constraints placed on their natural competitors in the housing finance and retail savings markets, the savings banks and the commercial banks. The savings banks were, in effect, part of the government and were allowed to have no lending function, all of the deposits they raised being handed over to the Exchequer. The rates of interest which they were allowed to pay to investors were also kept low and generally they were lethargic institutions. The commercial banks were subject to controls in the name of monetary policy, in particular, restrictions on the amount of their lending, and, in the 1970s, a restriction on the amount of their interest-bearing liabilities, known as 'the corset'. Gradually therefore the banks concentrated on offering a money transmission service only, and although they did offer deposit accounts these usually paid a lower rate of interest than comparable building society accounts. Similarly, the balance sheet constraints, and government exhortations to favour industry and commerce, prevented banks from lending as much on mortgages as they would have wished, so generally they became less concerned with the personal sector. With both banks and savings banks unable to compete effectively it was not surprising that building societies rapidly and effectively exploited the market opportunities open to them, and by 1980 had come to account for nearly 50 per cent of the liquid assets of the personal sector and some 80 per cent of outstanding mortgage loans.

Moreover, building societies achieved this by offering just these two basic services. They raised virtually no money from non-retail sources and they provided no loans other than for house purchase or improvement. Also, they provided virtually no additional services except those directly related to their mainstream business, for example, arrangement of property and life insurance. Cheque books, cash machines or other automated teller machine (ATM) facilities were conspicuous by their absence. This very simple nature of building society operations can be illustrated by looking at balance sheets and income and expenditure accounts. Unfortunately, detailed historic statistics on the source of building society funds are not available, but it is known that even in 1982 about 99 per cent of the funds invested with building societies were owned by individuals. Mortgage loans have traditionally accounted for about 80 per cent of assets, the remainder either being liquid assets, which have to be held in a range of government or government-guaranteed securities, or cash and bank deposits, and a limited amount of fixed assets.

The income of building societies has been almost entirely interest on their mortgage loans together with interest on their investments. There has been a limited amount of other income, largely insurance commission. However, mortgage and liquidity interest between them accounted for about 95 per cent of income received. Similarly, until the early 1980s over 90 per cent of expenditure of building societies was interest paid to their investors together with the tax paid on that interest. Management expenses were much lower than those of the banks, reflecting the very limited range of services offered by societies.

Over the past few years building society assets and liabilities and income and expenditure have begun to change. These changes reflect increasing competition in the mortgage and retail savings market from the banks which, in turn, contributed to greater competition between building societies themselves. Until the early 1980s societies had operated a powerful cartel which had controlled both investment and mortgage rates, and had yielded a sufficient profit to satisfy the vast majority of societies. The cartel, like other cartels, had diminished incentives to look for cheaper funds or ways of increasing income. The cartel, very often with support from both Labour and Conservative governments, had served to keep down the mortgage rate, and therefore the investment rate, and had led to a perpetual shortage of mortgage funds enabling a small number of generally smaller societies, if they so wished, to charge a mortgage rate higher than normal and to be certain of getting business at that higher rate.

Change came very quickly, between 1983 and 1985 in particular. The underlying causes of the change have probably been new technology, which has made entry into new markets comparatively easy, and the existence of a government committed to deregulation. In Britain the first cash dispensers were installed in 1967, and by the late 1970s these had become very sophisticated, enabling withdrawals to be made quickly, deposits to be made, and funds to be transferred between accounts. Increasingly powerful computer systems have also enabled non-traditional institutions to enter the money transmission market using clearing banks as agents to clear cheques. These twin forces led a number of institutions in the early 1980s to offer accounts both paying a high rate of interest and with ready access to funds through cheque books. The Co-operative Bank, operating primarily through Co-op stores, was one such institution, and the American Citibank was another. Unit trust groups and merchant banks also sought to provide such services. However, the missing link for most of them was the lack of access their customers had to cash, as all the ATMs were controlled by the commercial banks.

At about the same time (1980) the banks were freed from their balance sheet constraints and quickly became more orientated towards the retail market. By 1982 the banks were taking about 35 per cent of new mortgage business and significantly undercutting the mortgage rates charged by building societies, most of which imposed a higher rate of interest for larger loans. The building society cartel rapidly broke down under this external pressure and societies found themselves with mortgage rates determined not by collective decision making, but rather by the market. Competition for retail funds intensified and there was leapfrogging between societies. As societies found their margin increasingly under pressure so they had to look at other sources of income. Other institutions (including the major banks) began to offer interest-bearing money transmission accounts, and societies had to consider adding money transmission to the higher rates of interest which they already offered. As the price of retail funds was bid well above the price of wholesale funds so the wholesale markets looked increasingly attractive as a source of funds. Societies were assisted here by a government sympathetic to deregulation, and the necessary changes in the tax regulations enabling societies to tap the wholesale markets were quickly implemented.

As a result, by late 1985 a clear trend had been established for building societies to become more integrated into the more general financial markets. Increasingly they were competing with commercial banks to offer money transmission facilities, and instead of simply collecting savings and then deciding how to allocate them the task became one of liability management – that is, of lending to meet demand, but at a reasonable rate of interest, and then deciding how the increase in assets should be funded either through the retail or wholesale markets. These changes have begun to show through gently in balance sheets but more substantially in income and expenditure accounts. The amount of investors' funds held in wholesale form increased from 2 per cent at the end of 1982 to 4.3 per cent at the end of 1984 and a figure estimated at about 7 per cent at the end of 1985. More importantly, the proportion of the increase in funds obtained from wholesale sources was as high as 20 per cent in 1985. The increasing attractiveness of wholesale funds can be illustrated by looking at prevailing rates of interest in October 1985 when societies were empowered to use the Eurobond market for the first time. Those societies which went into this market could raise funds at little more than 11.75 per cent, at which time their retail funds were costing them at least one percentage point more at the margin.

No precise figures are available for building societies' accounts which offer money transmission facilities. However, the two largest societies were at the end of 1985 offering cheque book accounts (although the Halifax had announced the withdrawal of its scheme to new customers) and four other societies also offered cheque book accounts indirectly through links with banks. A number of other societies are offering more limited bill-paying facilities. The largest society, the Halifax, had a wide ATM network by the end of 1985 and by mid-1986 most societies were offering ATM facilities, largely through two shared networks. Societies have also expanded the range of other financial services which they offer, in particular foreign currency services.

Generally, the increasing proportion of all institutions' business that is done through ATMs, and the increasing use by building societies of wholesale funds, has implications for traditional branch networks. Those with a small number of staff, and this includes most building society branches, are capable of offering little more than a service involving the paying in and paying out of funds with a limited ability to sell investment accounts. As business increasingly by-passes branches so the economics of those branches begins to change, and to preserve their viability it becomes more necessary to offer a greater range of services through them. There has therefore been an increasing emphasis on fee income, both in specialist building society types of institution and in the commercial banks. There has also been an increasing need to cross-sell services, again taking advantage of High Street locations. House purchase is closely linked with many other services including, for example, conveyancing, estate agency, surveying, unsecured lending, insurance and insurance broking, all of which can be provided to some extent through High Street locations.

Table 4.2 illustrates the still fairly traditional nature of the building society balance sheet at the end of 1985, although the extent of the increase

Table 4.2 *Building Society Assets and Liabilities, 1980–5*

Liabilities	*1980*		*1985*		*Assets*	*1980*		*1985*	
	£m	*%*	*£m*	*%*		*£m*	*%*	*£m*	*%*
Shares	48,914	90.93	102,331	84.73	Mortgages	42,437	78.89	96,751	80.12
Deposits and loans	1,762	3.28	10,751	8.90	Cash and investments	10,606	19.71	22,699	18.80
Tax and other liabilities	1,229	2.28	2,772	2.30	Offices	622	1.16	997	0.83
					Other assets	128	0.24	317	0.26
General reserves	1,888	3.51	4,910	4.07					
Total	53,793	100.00	120,764	100.00	Total	53,793	100.00	120,764	100.00

Source: Registry of Friendly Societies, 1985; BSA, 1986.

in deposits and loans, which are mostly wholesale, is apparent. Table 4.3 illustrates the changing composition of the income and expenditure account over the five years up to 1985, showing the appearance of gross interest payments, mostly to wholesale investors.

Table 4.3 *Building Society Income and Expenditure, 1980–5*

		1980		*1985*
	£m	*£ per £100 mean assets*	*£m*	*£ per £100 mean assets*
Income				
Mortgage interest	5,913	11.88	12,022	10.76
Investment and bank interest	1,072	2.15	2,137	1.91
Investment profits (net of losses)	73	0.15	66	0.06
Commission	98	0.20	253	0.23
Rent	13	0.03	26	0.02
Other income (net)	6	0.01	31	0.03
	7,175	14.42	14,535	13.01
Expenditure				
Management expenses	590	1.18	1,261	1.13
Interest paid net (including SAYE)	4,846	9.74	8,589	7.69
Income tax	1,372	2.76	2,898	2.59
Interest paid gross	–	–	532	0.48
Corporation tax	117	0.24	480	0.43
Total	6,925	13.92	13,760	12.32
Other items (net)	–3	–	26	0.02
Added to general reserves	247	0.50	801	0.72

Source: As for Table 4.2.
Note: Management expenses include depreciation and exceptional pension costs.

That building societies were departing from their traditional specialist role was recognized in a government Green Paper, *Building Societies: A New Framework*, published in July 1984, and then subsequently in the Building Societies Bill, published in December 1985. The Green Paper accepted that societies had to diversify in order to continue competing in an increasingly competitive market and it proposed a wide range of additional powers.

The Green Paper argued that these were in many ways a logical extension of building society business. It is envisaged that societies would be able to have up to 5 per cent of their commercial assets in unsecured loans. The Green Paper also recognized the need for societies to provide money transmission services, and for specific powers to be given to overcome the legal problems that prevented societies from offering a full service. Specific authorization to offer services including money transmission, foreign currency services, insurance broking, estate agency, conveyancing and acting as agents for payments were in the Building Societies Bill, which was introduced in parliament in December 1985.

When the Bill was enacted building societies were freed to compete in a retail banking market with banks and other non-traditional participants. The general expectation is that the large societies will become full-scale retail 'banks' offering a full range of services, such that their customers will not also require bank accounts. Societies are also likely to use their data banks and computer facilities to cross-sell services. This applies, in particular, to insurance, which can be targeted at particular income or socio-economic groups. The large societies therefore are likely to generate an increasing proportion of their income through fees, rather than through the interest margin.

The regional and local societies will probably continue in their traditional role, trading strongly on their local connections, and perhaps linking with each other or other institutions to provide at least the core retail banking service, and perhaps other limited services.

The Act makes specific provision for building societies to convert to company status, and it is likely that some will do so, so as to be able to diversify more widely than the new Act will allow; but others may be encouraged to do so by financial institutions looking for a network of High Street outlets and seeing the acquisition of a building society as a suitable route. Among such institutions would be British banks without a national branch network, American banks and insurance companies.

The Act also provides for building societies to raise a maximum of 20 per cent of their funds from non-retail sources, a huge increase from the actual figure of 7 per cent at the end of 1985. Again, this is in recognition of the fact that wholesale funds can, at times, be substantially cheaper than retail funds, and that if building societies are unable to tap the wholesale market then they will be at a competitive disadvantage with other participants in the mortgage market. Indeed, in the past year or so there has been another surge in bank lending and also the advent of new institutions raising their funds entirely on a wholesale basis. Whether the 20 per cent figure will be adequate for long remains to be seen (there is provision in the Act for the figure to be increased to 40 per cent).

In general, although the new Act will require societies to have over 90 per cent of their commercial assets in mortgage loans, this will not require them to have over 90 per cent of their business in this category. It is perfectly possible for an institution to have 90 per cent of its assets, but only 1 per cent of its business, in a certain area. Even if building societies continue to dominate the housing finance market those societies will be quite different institutions from the ones that existed in the 1970s and early 1980s.

Specialist Housing Finance Deposit-Takers in Other Countries

The point has been made that building society types of institution also exist in other countries. This section briefly gives details of such institutions. South Africa is most similar to Britain in having a housing finance market dominated by the societies. The eleven societies account for some 70 per cent of outstanding mortgage debt, and largely raise their funds from the personal sector. However, they have made greater use of institutional money than British building societies.

South African building societies are more advanced than their British counterparts in respect of money transmission services; in particular, they have been offering ATM facilities for some years. Consideration is currently being given to new building society legislation, which will enable societies to diversify more widely and also to convert from mutual to company status. It is expected that most of the larger societies will elect to convert, although unlike the British ones they will probably continue to be building societies.

In Australia the permanent building societies are very similar to societies in Britain. However, they have a much smaller market share, accounting for a little under 40 per cent of the mortgage market. The savings banks have the largest market share with over 50 per cent. Australian building society legislation is borrowed from British legislation and the societies have operated in a very similar way, raising almost all their funds from the personal sector and lending largely for owner-occupation. The Australian financial system has recently been subject to a detailed scrutiny by two government committees and generally the system is being deregulated. Controls on bank interest rates have been removed and building societies are being given wider asset powers, including the power to lend unsecured. The second largest building society, the NSW Permanent, has recently converted to savings bank status.

The New Zealand building societies play a comparatively small role in the mortgage market. The major lender is the government-owned Housing Corporation. Again, the societies are very similar to their British counterparts, raising their funds from the retail sector and making loans on mortgage. They too have been given wider powers, in particular, to lend unsecured.

Developments in the United States illustrate the declining role for specialist housing finance institutions. Until perhaps ten years ago savings and loan associations were almost equivalent to British building societies. Most were mutual, although some had had a stock status for several years, and they raised their funds almost entirely through retail deposits. However, the American financial system was also highly regulated. In particular, institutions were not enabled to lend at variable rates and also their activities were confined to within state borders. The system worked quite well until interest rates began to increase markedly. There was an outflow of funds from institutions and as a result they were gradually freed from interest rate controls on their deposits. However, they were not similarly freed in respect of loans until 1982, when they were given a general power to make adjustable rate loans.

The industry was by this time in such a poor state that it was felt necessary to provide a very much wider range of powers in the hope that this might offset the losses being incurred on more traditional business. The Depository Institutions Deregulation and Monetary Control Act of 1980 sought to remove the remaining interest rate ceilings which had given savings associations a competitive advantage over banks, but in reality had done little more than allow non-regulated institutions, such as money market mutual funds, to enter the market. In exchange, savings associations were given wider powers including authorization to issue interest-bearing chequebook accounts, authorization to invest up to 20 per cent of assets in consumer loans, corporate debt securities and commercial paper, and authority to issue credit cards and engage in trust operations. In 1982 came the more far reaching Garn/St Germain Depository Institutions Act, which provided for the phasing out of all remaining interest rate controls by 1986, gave expanded authority to invest in consumer, commercial and agriculture loans and other investments, and permitted investment in tangible personal property for lease or sale of up to 10 per cent of total assets.

Perhaps more importantly, in the long term, the Act also considerably eased the requirements for institutions to convert from mutual to stock status, and it introduced a new category of institution, federal savings banks. Almost all the large institutions have now converted to stock status and have raised substantial capital sums on the way. Many have also converted to the federal savings bank charter which gives them an even greater ability to diversify, and effectively the distinction between savings associations and savings banks has been abolished. This has been recognized, for example, in the merging of trade associations representing the two groups, and the industry's statistics now generally group together new federal savings banks together with the old savings and loan associations.

There has been a great increase in the proportion of income generated from fees as opposed to the interest margin. Other income accounted for just 5.7 per cent of operating income in 1975, but by 1983 the proportion had risen to 18 per cent, and in 1984 it was 23 per cent.

It is clear from this brief survey that there is a worldwide trend for specialist housing finance deposit-takers to diversify both in respect of the funds which they raise, but more importantly in the services which they provide. It is no longer sufficient simply to pay a high rate of interest on savings because this will no longer attract adequate funds. Strong competition for mortgage business is forcing all institutions to offer a range of related services.

Savings Banks

Building societies can be regarded as a special type of savings bank. If one had to define the characteristics of a savings bank it would be an institution which raises its funds predominantly from retail sources, and to the extent that it makes loans these are largely to personal customers. The basic difference between a savings bank and a building society is that the latter has perhaps 80 per cent of its assets in mortgage loans whereas for savings banks the proportion is likely to be lower, typically perhaps 50 per cent although with a fairly wide range from about 20 per cent to 70 per cent. In many countries savings banks are owned by national governments or state governments and often they are linked together through central giro institutions which in many cases have become powerful institutions in their own right. This is true in particular of the West German *Landesbanken.*

Savings banks are often better placed than building societies to respond to market developments, in particular, the need to offer a wider range of services. This is because they have always offered a range of services and generally have been competitive with commercial banks in the market for money transmission services. What has held back the savings banks in some countries has been their control by government which has stifled innovation and restricted the growth of the sector.

In some countries savings banks have largely confined themselves to the personal sector, but in others they also lend to the corporate sector. It is not possible to restrict a service to corporate customers to the domestic market. If a corporate customer has an export or import business it will obviously require foreign currency services and if the savings bank itself cannot provide these then the probability is that the entire banking function will be shifted to a commercial bank. A typical pattern has been for savings banks to provide such services not directly, but rather through central giro institutions, although some of the larger savings banks have also moved into such fields directly.

The role of savings banks in providing housing finance loans can best be illustrated by looking at a number of countries. As stated above, in Australia savings banks account for over 50 per cent of the mortgage market. The largest savings bank, and the single largest mortgage lender in Australia, is the Commonwealth Savings Bank owned by the federal government. The second largest is the State Bank of Victoria, owned by the State of Victoria, and it is the largest deposit-taking institution and mortgage lender in that state. The commercial banks also own savings banks, and these are the next three largest mortgage lenders. Typically the savings banks have a little under 50 per cent of their assets in housing loans, most of the remaining assets being securities. They lend very little to industry or commerce. Table 4.4 shows the balance sheet of the Commonwealth Savings Bank as at June 1985.

Table 4.4 *The Balance Sheet of the Commonwealth Savings Bank as at June 1985*

Liabilities	*$m*	%	*Assets*	*$m*	%
Deposits	12,004	91	Housing loans	6,433	49
Capital and reserves	817	6	Other loans	893	7
Other liabilities	453	3	Financial assets	5,138	39
			Fixed assets	616	5
			Other assets	176	1
Total	13,255	100	Total	13,255	100

Source: Commonwealth Banking Corporation, 1985.

In France the savings banks account for about a quarter of the housing finance market, and about half of the personal savings market. There are well over 400 savings banks, all of which are local. In addition to making direct housing loans they also invest a significant proportion of their funds with their regulatory body, the Caisse des Depots et Consignations (CDC), which in turn finances rented housing and which makes assisted house purchase loans.

In West Germany the savings banks are major financial institutions. They are public sector bodies and operate in local areas only. At the end of 1983 there were 592 banks with over 17,000 offices. The savings banks have moved well beyond the personal sector and offer a range of services to corporate bodies. Personal deposits account for about 50 per cent of their liabilities and housing loans for about 25 per cent of their assets.

However, savings banks have a much bigger role in the housing finance market than these figures would suggest. In each of the German states there are central giro institutions known as *Landesbanken* which are largely owned by the savings banks. These in turn have subsidiary mortgage banks and *Bausparkassen* (specialist housing finance institutions which work on the contract system which is discussed in Chapter 6), which are the other main participants in the housing finance market. The savings bank often introduces business to these two institutions and may well make part of the loan package which is typically arranged for the original borrower. This point is considered in more detail in Chapter 6, but it is sufficient to note here this fairly wide-ranging role for the savings banks, which have the retail customers and which are therefore able to introduce business to other institutions, particularly mortgage banks which obtain their funds other than from individuals.

The savings banks also play a significant role in many other European countries, in particular Italy and Spain. A number of European countries also have co-operative banks which share some characteristics with savings banks. These co-operative banks generally have an agricultural base. They are strong in France where they are linked together through the Crédit

Agricole, one of the largest banks in the world, in Germany where they are linked nationally through one of the largest German banks, the DG Bank, and in the Netherlands through the Rabobank system. Although they have their agricultural base, as agriculture has taken a declining proportion of national income so they have diversified and now offer the full range of retail financial facilities. In the Netherlands the Rabobank is the largest single house purchase lender, and in France the Crédit Agricole is one of the major market participants with some 20 per cent of the total market. In West Germany the co-operative banks directly have only about 9 per cent of the housing finance market, but like the savings banks they have a more important role through the DG Bank, which owns the largest single mortgage bank, and which also owns one of the two largest *Bausparkassen*.

In some of the smaller European countries there is often a dominant savings bank institution, which is the largest single house purchase lender and generally owned or controlled by the state. Thus in Portugal the Caixa Geral de Depositós is the largest single financial institution and by far the largest lender for house purchase. Loans on retail estate generally, most of which are for house purchase, account for over a quarter of its assets. In Belgium the Caisse Generale D'Epargne et de Retraite is a state-owned and controlled institution which dominates both the retail savings market and the housing finance market.

It is clear from this brief international survey that in countries where savings banks are strong institutions operating independently, they are significant house purchase lenders. This is true in Australia, Italy and Spain. In countries where savings banks are linked together through central giro institutions which have subsidiary financial institutions, the savings banks have the more important role as acting as the retail interface between potential house buyers and those with access to funds, and often may have only a relatively small part of the activity on their own balance sheets.

Commercial Banks

Commercial banks differ in their retail business. There are some very large American commercial banks, for example, Morgan Guaranty and Bankers Trust, which have virtually no retail banking business at all. At the other extreme some commercial banks raise the bulk of their deposits from individuals and make a substantial proportion of loans to individuals. The British commercial banks are nearer to the retail end of the spectrum, and their branch networks are among the largest in the world.

However, this does not mean that they can be classified as institutions which rely on taking retail deposits, because these are now only a small proportion of the funds of the British commercial banks. At the end of 1985 the four big commercial banks in Britain had between 18 and 28 per cent of their deposits in the form of savings deposits, the remaining deposits being demand deposits and wholesale deposits. Another analysis shows that at this time about 41 per cent of the sterling deposits of the London and Scottish clearing banks were raised from persons, households and individual trusts. Over the years the banks have tended to raise a smaller proportion of their funds from savings deposits and a higher proportion from the wholesale markets, for example, between 1980 and 1985 the proportion of its deposits classified by Barclays as retail fell from 33 per cent to 18 per cent.

As noted earlier, for most of the 1960s and 1970s the British commercial banks were restrained from competing as much as they would wish because of balance sheet constraints operated in pursuance of monetary policy. This helps to explain why they declined as retail institutions, losing market share in the retail savings market and becoming almost non-existent in the mortgage market. When those constraints were finally removed in 1980 the banks fought back in the retail markets and now have become significant mortgage lenders in Britain, accounting for 17 per cent of outstanding mortgage balances. By coincidence their mortgage lending also accounts for about 17 per cent of their outstanding sterling assets.

Mortgage business is attractive for the commercial banks not just because it can be very profitable in its own right, but also because it gives the opportunity to bring in related business from the other services which the banks offer, in particular unsecured loans, bridging finance and insurance broking. One of the British commercial banks, Lloyds, has made a more direct entry into the housing finance market by establishing the largest chain of estate agents in the country. The agents can help introduce business to Lloyds Bank and in turn the bank can introduce business to the estate agents.

In Britain the commercial banks provide housing finance directly, although one of the banks operates through a wholly owned subsidiary but this is not altogether apparent to the customer. In some other countries the commercial banks instead own specialist housing finance institutions to which they can introduce business and from which business can be introduced to them.

Brief details of the involvement of commercial banks in the housing finance market in other countries are as follows:

(1) In the USA commercial banks have about 15 per cent of outstanding mortgage loans. The largest bank in the housing finance market is the Bank of America, the second largest American bank, which is probably one of the five largest housing finance lenders in the country. The second largest bank lender, Citicorp, not only lends on its own account, but more recently it has acquired four specialist savings associations. The motivation for this has partly been to overcome limitations on inter-state activity. All of the institutions were financially unsound and Citicorp purchased them as a means to

breaking into new markets rather than because it particularly wished to operate through subsidiary organizations. Most of the large commercial banks have mortgage bank subsidiaries which originate and service loans held by other institutions.

(2) In Australia the main trading banks have about 10 per cent of the housing finance market directly, but all play a greater role through their ownership of savings banks. The Commonwealth Savings Bank, mentioned earlier in this chapter, is part of the Commonwealth Banking Corporation. The three large commercial banks all own savings banks each of which are larger house purchase lenders than any of the specialist building societies.

(3) In West Germany the 'big banks', as they are known, do very little direct house purchase lending. However, they do play an important role through their ownership of mortgage banks and they also have connections with the private *Bausparkassen*. The largest of the German banks, the Deutsche Bank, is probably the single largest house purchase lender in Germany.

(4) In Canada the chartered banks have been rapidly increasing their share of mortgage lending and now account for about 40 per cent of the market. They have a similar proportion of the market for savings deposits.

5 The Mortgage Bank System

The previous chapter showed that the deposit-taking system of housing finance operated through just one stage of financial intermediation: individual savings are invested with deposit-taking institutions which in turn make loans for house purchase. The mortgage bank system involves at least two stages of intermediation. The institutions which make mortgage loans do not raise their funds directly from the retail sector, but rather raise money from the professional money and capital markets, which in turn attract much of their funds from the retail sector. Mortgage banks (the term is used in its widest sense here) have to work with the retail sector to obtain and service their mortgage business. However, there are many variations on the mortgage bank system, largely depending on the form of ownership of the institution. There are also many ways in which wholesale funds can be raised.

In recent years the sharp division between the deposit-taking system and the mortgage bank system has broken down as predominantly retail institutions have made greater use of wholesale funds while mortgage banks have forged stronger links with the retail sector.

Types of Mortgage Bank and Methods of Raising Funds

A mortgage bank can be defined very simply as an institution which makes loans for house purchase but which raises its funds from the capital and money markets rather than from the retail savings market. Some 'mortgage banks' use those words in their title and others do not, and indeed some institutions may operate simultaneously as a mortgage bank and a retail bank. The type of ownership of a mortgage bank may well determine how it raises its funds and how it operates.

At one end of the mortgage bank spectrum are the government-owned mortgage banks. Examples include the State Housing Bank in Norway, the Crédit Foncier in France, the Mortgage Bank of Spain, and the Government Housing Loan Corporation in Japan. A number of developing countries also have such institutions. This analysis concentrates on the position in industrialized countries.

Government mortgage banks are in a very different position from private sector institutions in terms of raising funds. They do not need to establish their credit-worthiness and therefore are able to borrow at the cheapest rates. In a number of countries, for example, New Zealand, the mortgage banks obtain their funds partly through budgetary allocations.

Government-owned mortgage banks may well operate on a non-market principle. Indeed, it is difficult to think of a logical reason why there should be a government-owned mortgage bank operating on market principles. Mortgage banks may, for example, be the instrument through which subsidies are allocated. This is true of the Crédit Foncier in France and of the Housing Corporation of New Zealand.

Alternatively, governments may require financial institutions to purchase a specified quantity of bonds issued by its mortgage bank, or by private mortgage banks. This has occurred, for example, in Sweden, where financial institutions have been obliged to purchase what are called priority bonds from the government and the mortgage banks. The funds obtained are used to finance cheap house purchase. In Italy, until recently, financial institutions were obliged to purchase certain quantities of bonds issued by the special mortgage credit institutions. The general tendency has been for there to be a movement away from such rigid direction of funds.

The one problem that government mortgage banks inevitably have is how they make contact with potential borrowers. If they are operating on a non-market basis there is no problem, because there will always be a demand for a subsidized product and they will not have difficulty in lending. Where, however, they are operating more on a market basis, then it is essential that they link with retail financial institutions.

The second group of mortgage banks are those that are part of wider financial groups. These mortgage banks may obtain their mortgage business from other institutions within the group. The best examples here are the mortgage banks in West Germany. The private sector mortgage banks are largely owned by the commercial banks. They raise funds independently on the capital markets, but they obtain their customers through references from their parent commercial banks. The public sector mortgage banks are part of the comprehensive savings bank sector in each state. The savings banks jointly own the regional girobank which in turn has a mortgage bank subsidiary. The mortgage bank is able to obtain its business through references from the savings banks. In the case of West Germany most home-buyers have a package of loans which includes a loan from the retail institution with which the individual has contact, a long-term loan from a related mortgage bank, and a *Bausparkasse* contract from the related *Bausparkasse*. This package system is considered in the next chapter.

Where mortgage banks are part of a wider financial grouping they can often obtain direct funding from their parent institution. Such funding may take the form of long-term loans together with short-term finance as necessary. Among the institutions that operate in this way are the Union de Crédit pour le Bâtiment in France, which is part of the Compagnie Bancaire group, and the mortgage bank subsidiary of the Rabobank in the Netherlands. However, direct financing of this type is likely to be only one of a number of sources of finance.

Finally, there are independent mortgage banks which have no connection with other financial groupings. Denmark is the best example, where three mortgage banks provide almost all house purchase finance in the country. Sweden also has a very large independent mortgage bank which has some 50 per cent of the market for house purchase loans. These banks may raise funds either on an unsecured basis or, effectively, backed by mortgage loans, either generally or specifically. Funds raised in this way will normally have the same maturity as the corresponding house purchase loans and the mortgage bank has the difficult task of ensuring adequate matching of assets and liabilities. For the institutional investor the specific linking of individual mortgage loans and bonds through which funds are raised is inconvenient, even if there is a guarantee, which there generally has to be. One problem is early repayment. If this is allowed then it may be inconvenient for the investor and, indeed, if interest rates are falling it can be positively disadvantageous to him. If early redemption is not allowed then the borrower may be placed in a difficult position if he wishes to move house.

Instruments for Raising Wholesale Funds

A number of instruments can be used to raise wholesale funds. Obviously, a mortgage bank will want to raise funds on a long-term basis, because its loans are predominantly long term. However, it may need a certain amount of short-term funds for day-to-day management of finances. In some cases short-term funds can be continually rolled over into what is effectively long-term finance. Short-term funds can be raised through time deposits and instruments such as certificates of deposit. A time deposit is very similar to the retail accounts which many institutions offer, with a specified rate of interest being offered for a deposit for a specified period. The main difference compared with retail deposits is that the amount is substantially larger. The term is often between three months and one year. Certificates of deposit are more attractive to some institutional investors in that they are marketable, and therefore if the investor wants his money back immediately he can obtain it without waiting for the instrument to mature.

Increasing use has been made of certificates of deposit to fund house purchase loans in the recent past, but, paradoxically perhaps, not by mortgage banks. These short-term instruments are an alternative method of raising funds for retail deposit-takers in that their liabilities are typically short term and rates of interest are variable. If a mortgage bank makes long-term loans at fixed rates of interest then short-term deposits in large quantities are not a sound method of finance.

The point has already been made that where a mortgage bank is part of a wider financial grouping, it can obtain its funding through long-term loans from other parts of the group. Such funding will normally be on a commercial basis, although obviously the interest margin on the loan by the lending part of the institution is effectively for the benefit of the whole group. Some method has to be found of establishing an equitable rate of interest at which such financing takes place. The loans will need to be long term, generally at fixed rates of interest, although recently increasing use has been made of variable rate loans.

The traditional method of funding for mortgage banks is through mortgage bonds and this is the method which is largely used by independent mortgage banks. There are two ways in which mortgage bonds can be issued. The first, and the most common, is for a mortgage bank to issue a large tranche of bonds for, say, a ten-year period, with a fixed rate of interest. The mortgage bank will then endeavour to make corresponding mortgage loans, also for a ten-year period, and also at a fixed rate of interest, slightly above the rate of interest which it is paying on the mortgage bonds. There is therefore an exact matching of assets and liabilities. Depending on the status of the mortgage bank it may need to offer security, with effectively the mortgage loans as a pool backing the mortgage bonds, but in some cases it may be possible to issue bonds on an unsecured basis. Where funds are being raised in this way then the mortgage bank has to guard itself against premature redemption of its loans in the event of interest rates falling, as otherwise it will be committed to paying a high rate of interest on the long-term bonds with no guarantee of being able to obtain adequate income from its mortgage loans.

The second, and somewhat old-fashioned, method is for the house purchaser to be given bonds which he sells in the open market. The payments which he makes on his mortgage loan are used directly to fund the holders of the bonds, although obviously the mortgage bank plays the role of intermediary. This method is used in Denmark. The mortgage bank has virtually no risk in that, for example, it does not even have to hold the proceeds of bond issues for a short time until it makes the loans. The institutional investor has the security of the mortgage but there is the risk of premature redemption. This can be guarded against by a high redemption fee, and in Denmark if a borrower wants to redeem his loan he has to buy back the bonds. If he had taken out a loan at a rate of interest of, for example, 20 per cent and market rates fell to 10 per cent then to buy back the bonds he would have to pay twice as much as the amount of the loan.

Mortgage banks have recently been able to make use of new financial instruments, deriving partly from the internationalization of the capital markets. The volume of syndicated loans has increased considerably. Syndicated loans occur when a number of banks co-operate to make one loan, therefore sharing the risk, and can be more attractive to a bank than making a large loan on its own. The rate of interest that syndicated loans will attract obviously depends on the credit-worthiness of the mortgage bank.

The Eurobond market has also become increasingly attractive. This is a market through which the funds are raised outside the country of the issuer. Funds can be raised in various currencies. The major currency has been dollars, and American institutions have been able to raise substantial funds on the Euromarket from financial and other institutions in Europe and Japan which wish to have assets denominated in dollars. Funds are normally raised in large amounts, and a number of investment banks have become specialists in making and dealing in Eurobond issues. The market is becoming increasingly sophisticated, in particular through the use of swap arrangements by which funds can be raised in one currency and converted into another, or raised at fixed rates of interest and converted into variable rates. As the market has become more sophisticated so the margin over money market rates of interest at which funds can be attracted has been lowered substantially.

Again, funds can be raised on the Eurobond market, either secured or unsecured depending on the credit-worthiness of the issuing institutions. It may be noted in passing that, somewhat paradoxically, mutual deposit-taking institutions, such as British and Australian building societies, are better placed to raise funds on the Eurobond market than mortgage banks. This is because Eurobonds, and indeed wholesale instruments generally, must always rank before the retail deposits of a building society where these are held in the form of shares. A British building society would have to lose nearly 90 per cent of its assets before the holders of any unsecured deposit would be at risk, whereas for a bank the proportion is nearer to 8 per cent or 7 per cent. Mutual institutions in particular are therefore able to raise substantial sums at very fine margins on the Eurobond market, but strong mortgage banks can also raise funds in a similar way. Where the issuing authority is a government agency then again it can obtain funds at a very fine rate. The Crédit Foncier, the government-owned mortgage bank in France, and two American secondary mortgage institutions, the Federal Home Loan Mortgage Corporation and the Federal National Mortgage Association, both of which can offer a US-government guarantee, have made substantial use of the Eurobond markets. Where it is necessary to offer security, mortgages can be used for this purpose and a number of American savings associations have raised funds on the Eurobond market backed by specific pools of mortgages. This is possible for American institutions because in the USA there is a secondary mortgage market for which mortgage loans have to meet certain criteria, for example, in respect of valuation and loan-to-value and loan-to-income ratios, and must also have either private or government insurance.

The rates of interest on money market instruments are generally higher than those on retail instruments. However, the cost of raising wholesale funds is substantially less than that of raising retail funds. For example, the cost of raising a large Eurobond loan will be under 0.01 per cent a year. By contrast, the cost of operating a savings account is likely to be about 1 per cent a year, and the cost of operating a full retail banking current account is likely to be nearer 10 per cent a year. Thus one of the basic differences between the mortgage bank system and the deposit-taking system is that the former raises funds at a higher cost than the latter but with lower management expenses. In fact, in many countries, particularly Britain, there are times when the cost of retail funds has been substantially above that of wholesale funds, the end of 1985 being a good example. The interest rates paid and charged by deposit-taking institutions are much stickier than money market rates with the result that when rates rise rapidly the rates of interest at which the deposit-taking institutions operate tend to lag behind. But the same applies when rates fall. The borrower from a mortgage bank cannot therefore be isolated from the vagaries of the money markets.

Mortgage Bank Operations

A major characteristic of the mortgage bank system is that loans have largely been made at fixed rates of interest. This has been necessary because until recently long-term funds had to be raised at fixed rates of interest simply because variable rate instruments did not exist in sufficient quantity. Operating on fixed rates would seem to avoid the dangers of borrowing short and lending long. Indeed, it does so while interest rates are comparatively stable. The mortgage bank system has worked very effectively in West Germany where long-term interest rates have moved in a very narrow range. However, fixed rates are not without their problems. Potential house buyers might hold off buying and therefore obtaining mortgage loans until mortgage rates fall, and this can lead to substantial cyclical fluctuations in mortgage bank activity. When interest rates fall there will be an increased demand for loans and possibly a wish on the part of some borrowers with high rates to redeem their loans prematurely, a point which has already been noted. They cannot be allowed to do so without putting the mortgage bank at risk.

Increasingly, the problems of long-term fixed rate loans have been recognized (a point considered in more detail in Chapter 8) and mortgage banks have moved towards more frequent changes in rates of interest. This process has been taken furthest in Italy where long-term mortgage loans made by mortgage banks now have interest rates fixed for six months at a time and bonds are issued on similar terms. In other countries it has become common for the maximum maturity of bonds to be five years and for loans to be at fixed rates for five years at a time. As greater use is made of long-term floating instruments so one would expect even greater variability in the interest rates charged by mortgage banks. This marks a significant bringing together of the retail and mortgage bank systems, at least as far as the customer is concerned. Both increasingly operate with variable rather than fixed rates of interest.

The other special feature of mortgage bank operations has already been touched on, and that concerns the source of their mortgage business. A retail bank, whether general or more specialist, has no problems in this respect because it has a wide customer base and it also has an established branch network. A mortgage bank will have no retail customer base and no branches. It therefore needs to get its business by linking with other institutions in the market. The point has already been made that where mortgage banks are part of wider financial groupings they can obtain business from other parts of the group, especially the retail bank parts, and West Germany was cited as the best example here. Other countries where this is true include Italy and Israel. Where the mortgage banks are independent they need to establish links either with retail banks or further downstream with real estate agents and housebuilders. Sweden provides an example of where links exist with retail financial institutions. The largest mortgage lender is the Urban Mortgage Bank, a mutual institution. This obtains its funds largely through priority bond issues which financial institutions are obliged to purchase. For various reasons the commercial and savings banks have not been able to make long-term mortgage loans, so they have referred business to the Urban Mortgage Bank. Any institution obtaining its funds in this way is vulnerable to a change in financial policy in respect of priority bonds or in respect of the removal of limitations on savings or commercial banks from making mortgage loans. The Urban Mortgage Bank in Sweden is in this position and is having to change its method of operation quite considerably.

The second alternative is to establish links with the real estate agents and housebuilders. Denmark and France provide good examples here. In France the largest independent mortgage bank, the Union de Crédit pour le Bâtiment, is partly owned by the representative organization of housebuilders in France and it obtains much of its business through direct references from builders. It also has many agents who are real estate brokers. In Denmark, the three mortgage banks obtain their business directly from introductions through real estate agents.

The method of working of the various mortgage banks is considered in more detail in the final sections of this chapter.

The Mortgage Bank System in Denmark

The Scandinavian countries generally rely heavily on the mortgage bank system for the provision of loans for house purchase. This is particularly true in Denmark, where the residential mortgage market is dominated by three mortgage banks: Kreditforeningen Danmark (the Mortgage Credit Association, Denmark); Nykredit (the New Danish Mortgage Credit Association); and Byggeriets Realkreditfond (the Housing Mortgage Fund).

Table 5.1 *Mortgage Credit Institutions, Denmark, Assets and Liabilities, 30 November 1985*

Liabilities	*DKrm*	%	*Assets*	*DKrm*	%
Bonds in circulation	520,829	91	Mortgages	426,860	75
			Cash loans	103,535	18
Index-linked charge	6,962	1	Bonds	31,930	6
			Cash	3,204	1
Other liabilities	6,994	1	Commitments by guarantors	1,987	–
Guarantee capital	1,987	–	Property	332	–
Reserves	35,153	6	Other	4,077	1
Total	571,925	100	Total	571,925	100

Source: Realkreditradet, 1986, Table 11.

Table 5.2 *Mortgage Credit Institutions, Denmark, Income and Expenditure, Year to 30 November 1985*

	DKrm	*DKr per 100 DKr mean assets*
Income		
Interest on mortgages and cash loans	44,565	8.37
Index-linked appreciation	1,238	0.23
Interest on bond holdings	3,647	0.68
Contribution to reserves	887	0.17
Fees	199	0.04
Total	50,536	9.49
Expenditure		
Interest on bonds	44,695	8.39
Administration	1,417	0.27
Index-linked appreciation	1,238	0.23
Mortgage losses	524	0.09
Total	47,874	8.98
Profit	2,662	0.50

Source: Realkreditradet, 1986, Table 10.

The mortgage banks obtain their funds through fixed rate bond issues over twenty-five or thirty years. Loans are made on a similar basis. The main purchasers of mortgage bonds are the pension funds, banks and insurance companies.

Tables 5.1 and 5.2 show the balance sheet and the profit and loss account for the Danish mortgage banks for the year to 30 November 1985. Table 5.1 shows that liabilities are almost entirely bonds, with the addition, of course, of reserves. Because the mortgage banks do not face any withdrawals of funds, there is no need for them to hold significant liquid assets, nor do they need significant fixed assets, as they do not have branch networks. This is also illustrated in the income and expenditure account (Table 5.2), which shows very low administrative costs.

The mortgage banks obtain their business through links with other institutions in the housing market, in particular the real estate agents. These links are technologically advanced, and it is now possible for a real estate agent to originate a loan from his own office by electronic means.

The Mortgage Bank System in Other Countries

The final section of this chapter briefly sets out how the mortgage bank system is used in a number of other countries. Generally, the system is not used significantly in the English-speaking countries, but predominates elsewhere, especially in the continent of Europe.

France has a particularly complicated housing finance market, largely because of a number of government-approved loan schemes. The two largest single leaders are the Crédit Agricole, the network of agricultural co-operative banks, and the Crédit Foncier. The Crédit Foncier is a specialist government-controlled mortgage bank which also has certain supervisory functions in the mortgage market. It is not a deposit-taking body, but rather obtains all of its funds through bond issues and other long-term sources of funds. It makes long-term house purchase loans almost entirely under various government programmes. Generally, it can be considered as a non-market institution.

A more typical mortgage bank is the Union de Crédit pour le Bâtiment (UCB), which as noted earlier is part of the Compagnie Bancaire group. The Compagnie Bancaire owns 33 per cent of the share capital of UCB, the Crédit Foncier owns 21 per cent, and the National Building Federation owns 15 per cent. UCB obtains its funds through borrowing on the mortgage market, and through short-term borrowing from its parent bank. About 90 per cent of its assets are in the form of housing loans. The balance sheet for UCB at the end of 1985 is shown in Table 5.3.

UCB obtains its mortgage business through links with other agents in the housing market. It operates 70 agencies of its own, and has 230 exclusive agents and thousands of other agents, including 2,700 housing developers, 7,100 estate agents, 8,700 contractors and 3,600 lawyers.

In West Germany, the mortgage banks account for about 30 per cent of house purchase lending. They raise their funds through bearer and other long-term borrowing, and collectively have about 40 per cent of their assets

Table 5.3 *Union de Crédit pour le Bâtiment (France), Balance Sheet, End 1985*

Liabilities	*FFm*	*%*	*Assets*	*FFm*	*%*
Borrowing on mortgage market and other loans	42,200	73	Loans	51,080	89
			Other loans	2,195	4
			Provisions	1,341	2
			Property	162	–
Borrowing from banks	5,843	10	Liquid assets	738	1
			Other assets	2,036	4
Working finance	2,243	4			
Bonds	3,689	6			
Other liabilities	1,595	3			
Reserves	1,273	2			
Capital	709	1			
Total	57,552	100	Total	57,552	100

Source: UCB, 1986.

in long-term housing loans, most of the remaining assets being loans to public authorities. Almost all of the mortgage banks are linked with other financial institutions. There are twelve public mortgage banks, which are owned by the central giro institutions for the regional savings banks. They obtain their mortgage business through introductions from the savings banks, and often the mortgage bank loan is part of a package embracing a short-term savings bank loan and a *Bausparkasse* contract. The package concept is considered in detail in the next chapter. There are twenty-one private sector mortgage banks, most of which are owned by the commercial banks or insurance companies, and they obtain their business through their parent companies.

The Italian housing finance system imposes a division between institutions which can operate on a short-term basis and those which can operate on a long-term basis. There are about twenty special credit institutions which exist specifically to provide housing finance. All of these are either sections of banks, or corporate institutions owned by groups of banks. The two largest lenders are the special credit institutions of Cariplo, which is claimed to be the largest savings bank in the world, and that of the San Paolo Bank. Obviously they obtain their business through introductions from their parent banks. Unlike mortgage banks in most other countries, an increasing proportion of the business of the Italian special credit institutions has been at variable rates. Both the bonds and the mortgage loans are linked to money market rates on a six-monthly basis.

In Spain, the largest single lender is the government-owned Spanish Mortgage Bank. This obtains its funds largely through loans from the Official Credit Institute, a government body. It makes loans under a variety of government programmes, for rented accommodation as well as owner-occupied housing. More recently there has been a major reform of the housing finance system in Spain with the introduction of a mortgage market through which funds are raised for relatively short terms, between three and five years, at fixed rates of interest, and loans are made with rates of interest renewable at the appropriate interval.

In Norway, the largest single lender is the State Housing Bank. This mainly obtains its funds directly from the government rather than through market loans, and its lending is at heavily subsidized rates of interest.

Sweden, like Denmark, has a housing finance system based almost entirely on the mortgage bank system. The housing finance market in Sweden has been heavily influenced by government policy of credit controls and subsidizing mortgage loans. Loans are made at below-market rates of interest, and these are funded by priority housing bonds, which have to be purchased by the financial institutions. The largest single lender is the Urban Mortgage Bank, which has a special mutual type of constitution. It obtains its business through introductions from banks, which have been prevented from making mortgage loans directly because of credit controls. The savings banks and the commercial banks each own housing finance institutions, which operate in a similar way, and which obtain business from their parent institutions.

The financial markets in Sweden are in the process of being liberalized, and this is expected to lead to considerably increased activity in the mortgage market on the part of the commercial banks and the savings banks, at the expense of the housing finance institutes.

In Japan, the largest lender is the Government Housing Loan Corporation, with about a third of the market. This is the largest single housing finance institution in the world. It is a mortgage bank, and represents a good example of the double intermediation system. It obtains almost all of its funds from a government-owned body, the Trust Fund Bureau. This in turn obtains its funds from savings in the postal savings system, the largest single deposit-taking institution in the world. These savings have a tax benefit and therefore are acquired at a below-market rate of interest. In turn, the loans made by the Trust Fund Bureau to the Housing Loan Corporation are also at a below-market rate of interest and are then further subsidized by the government, enabling the Corporation to make relatively cheap housing loans. In fact, the Corporation does not lend money directly itself, but rather operates through approved financial institutions, largely banks, which act as agents.

6 The Contract System and Loan Packages

The contract system is a closed system in which potential borrowers themselves provide the funds through anticipatory savings. Because the system is closed, it can operate at below-market rates of interest. The contract system can never provide all of the funds which the house purchaser requires, and hence has to be used in tandem with one of the other systems. In practice, contract systems largely owe their existence to government subsidies of one form or another.

Theoretical Aspects

At first sight, the contract system has its attractions. Those who wish to borrow provide the necessary funds themselves through savings in anticipation of their need to borrow. The direct link between the saving and borrowing functions is therefore established, and the system can operate on mutual lines because in the long term the interests of investors and borrowers are identical, that is, participants are both investors and borrowers. The system can also operate on below-market rates of interest and this is what is particularly attractive about it to home buyers. Of course, it has to be paid for by the acceptance of a lower rate of interest on savings. However, the customer may not perceive it in this way, but rather may regard the cheap loan as more than counteracting the low rate of interest on savings.

The system is most suited to those countries where people purchase later on in life, and therefore where they have had an opportunity to build up a substantial deposit. This makes it inappropriate in a country like Britain, where people purchase their first homes at a very early age.

The main problem with the contract system is that even where house purchase is deferred it cannot raise all of the money which is required to fund the housing finance market. Chapter 1 showed how savings are held predominantly by the old, whereas loans are raised by the young. This can also be illustrated by looking at specific examples. Assume, for instance, a contract system in which loans are available after five years. If an individual saves £100 a month for five years, then with a 10 per cent rate of interest, he will have accumulated savings of £7,000. The £100 a month is a realistic savings amount for people in rented accommodation saving the deposit towards the purchase of their house. The £7,000 represents, of course, an average balance of only £3,500 over the five-year period. However, the investor may then want to borrow a total of perhaps £30,000 over twenty-five years; his borrowing requirement is some eight times the amount that he has saved.

The contract system deals with this particular problem in a number of ways. The most important solution is the recognition that the system cannot itself produce all of the funds which a house purchaser requires. It therefore has to be used in tandem with either the deposit-taking system, or the mortgage bank system, or indeed both, and typically can provide no more than a third of the loan which a house buyer needs.

The contract system benefits if people who do not actually want to obtain a loan can be encouraged to save. There will always be some who begin a contract with the intention of purchasing a home, but who for one reason or another do not actually borrow at the end of the day, and the deposits of those people can help fund the loans of others. In practice, however, contract systems always work with some government subsidy, and they may prove to be an extremely attractive savings scheme, for higher-rate tax-payers in particular. The more that those who do not actually want a loan can be encouraged to take out a savings contract, the more effectively the scheme will operate, but in turn this must require a great element of subsidy on the part of the government.

Another important feature of the contract system is that it continually needs new entrants in order to operate effectively. In practice, it is not the case that the savings of individuals are used to fund loans to those same individuals. Rather, those who are saving today are effectively providing the funds which are lent to those who have completed their savings contracts. The system therefore continually needs new entrants because if a contract system was closed down at any one time, then there would be a huge potential liability to those qualifying for mortgage loans, but no means of funding them.

A final feature of the contract system is that it is relatively inflexible. There normally needs to be a fairly simple mathematical relationship between the amount saved and the amount which can be borrowed, and loans will be available only after a set period of saving. This may be appropriate for some house purchasers, but it is not for all. This leads to the development of anticipatory loans, which house buyers may take out where they need to borrow to purchase a house but where they are not entitled to a loan on favourable terms under the contract system. The latter then becomes a method not of financing house purchase, but rather of paying off other loans which have been used to finance house purchase.

As already noted the deficiencies of the contract system mean that it is only widely used in those countries where there is a significant government subsidy, and, in effect, saving under the scheme carries advantages in its own right. The system is used extensively in only three industrialized countries – West Germany, France and Austria – in each case with high government subsidies and in conjunction with loans provided by other means: the state in Austria, and the savings bank and mortgage bank systems in West Germany and France.

The *Bausparkasse* System in West Germany

The contract system is longest established and most commonly used in West Germany. Specialist institutions, the *Bausparkassen*, are alone allowed to offer the building savings contracts. A person can contract for any amount and he has to agree to deposit a certain amount each year, generally 5 per cent of the agreed amount. The rate of interest received is either 2.5 per cent or 4.5 per cent a year depending on the plan chosen by the investor. Once 40 per cent or 50 per cent of the contractual sum has been saved, the person is then entitled to the entire contractual amount as a loan. This carries a rate of interest of either 4.5 per cent or 5.75 per cent, depending on which savings rate was selected. The government pays a substantial tax-free bonus on the amount saved during a year or alternatively offers a tax deduction in respect of contributions to a building savings contract.

Table 6.1 shows changes in *Bausparkassen* activity between 1973 and 1985. The changes in the number of new contracts can largely be attributed to changes in the level of government bonus. The level of bonus was reduced substantially in 1982, and it will be seen that the net increase in contracts has been substantially lower since that time.

Table 6.1 *Bausparkassen Activity, 1973–85*

Year	*Net increase in contracts 000*	*Contracts outstanding 000*	*Savings paid in DMm*	*Building loans made DMm*	*Total assets DMm*
1973		13,787	19,000	21,084	70,435
1974	1,189	14,976	19,052	18,028	77,686
1975	1,121	16,097	20,241	19,298	86,952
1976	1,241	17,338	22,070	21,404	94,906
1977	1,267	18,605	23,678	23,356	102,153
1978	1,285	19,890	25,707	25,903	111,223
1979	1,297	21,187	27,863	30,990	121,932
1980	1,477	22,664	27,437	31,220	132,501
1981	838	23,502	27,134	31,744	142,979
1982	310	23,812	25,610	20,756	149,655
1983	247	24,059	27,278	19,464	155,392
1984	234	24,293	24,585	20,560	160,937
1985	267	24,560	23,481	19,508	160,984

Source: Deutsche Bundesbank, 1983 and 1986a, Table 21.

Typically, a *Bausparkasse* loan will provide no more than one-third of the amount which the homebuyer requires. As noted in chapter 5 the remaining loan finance may well come from a mortgage bank loan together with a short-term loan from a savings bank or a co-operative bank. Here, the package element is important. The *Bausparkassen* are not fully independent institutions, but rather have strong connections with other financial institutions. There are thirteen public *Bausparkassen*, which are connected with the central giro institutions of the savings banks. They obtain their business through introductions from the savings banks. The mortgage bank subsidiaries of the central giro institutions will make the mortgage bank loan, and if further finance is needed then a short-term term savings bank loan will be made. Such loans can often be in anticipation of a *Bausparkasse* contract maturing, and here the cheap loan will be used to repay a more expensive, shorter-term loan.

The private *Bausparkassen* are largely owned by insurance companies and banks. There are two very large private *Bausparkassen*, each accounting for a little under 30 per cent of the total assets of all private *Bausparkassen*. The Beamtenkeim-Stattenwerk (BHW) is owned by the German Federation of Trades Unions and Civil Servants' Trade Union. The Schwaebisch Hall is owned by the co-operative banks and obtains its business through introductions from individual credit co-operatives.

Table 6.2 shows the assets and liabilities of *Bausparkassen* as at the end of 1985. It will be seen that liabilities are largely savings under contractual savings schemes, while 90 per cent of assets are building loans.

Table 6.2 *Bausparkassen, Assets and Liabilities, End 1985*

Liabilities	*DMm*	*%*	*Assets*	*DMm*	*%*
Deposits from non-banks under savings contracts	123,045	79	Building loans	139,169	90
Other deposits from non-banks	3,123	2	Other lending to non-banks	513	–
Deposits and borrowing from banks	15,045	10	Lending to banks	13,454	9
Provisions	2,771	2	Other assets	2,256	1
Capital	6,551	4			
Other liabilities	4,857	3			
Total	155,392	100	Total	155,392	100

Source: Deutsche Bundesbank, 1986b.

The French *Épargne-Logement* System

A contractual savings for house purchase scheme was introduced in France in 1965. Unlike in West Germany, there are no specialist institutions offering the scheme, but rather all institutions are free to offer it with the approval of the government. There are two variations of the scheme. The *plans d'épargne-logement* (housing savings plans) require an initial payment of FF1,500, and then regular payments not exceeding FF3,600 a year for five years. The maximum deposit which can be held in the plan is FF300,000. A rate of interest of 6.3 per cent a year is paid, and the government bonus is available up to FF10,000, which can increase the rate of interest up to 10 per cent. There is entitlement to a loan after three years, the loan amount being 2.5 times the amount saved. The maximum loan is FF400,000, and the rate of interest is 8.0 per cent.

The second variation is the *comptes d'épargne-logement* (housing savings accounts), which are more modest. The initial deposit is a maximum of FF750, and the minimum annual payment is FF150, with a total ceiling on deposits held in the account of FF100,000. The rate of interest paid is 3.25 per cent, and there is a bonus of a similar rate up to a ceiling of FF7,500. A loan can be obtained after eighteen months at 1.5 times the amount saved, but the maximum loan is FF150,000, while the rate of interest is 4.75 per cent.

Loans under the scheme generally provide only 40 per cent of the total loan finance required. As in West Germany, complementary loans are needed. There are special complementary housing savings loans, which carry a rate of interest fixed by the government, generally a little below market levels. Many borrowers also have free-market housing loans, or loans under the government-assisted scheme for subsidizing house purchase loans. The cost to the government of the savings bonus and tax exemptions is estimated at about £900 million in 1983 and the scheme is viable only because less than one-half of savers exercise their rights to a loan.

Table 6.3 shows the growth of housing savings accounts and plans. At the end of 1983 loans outstanding under the scheme were FF39.1 billion for

Table 6.3 *Housing Accounts and Plans, France, 1966–83*

End year	*Number of accounts*		*Cumulative net deposits*	
	Accounts 000	*Plans 000*	*Accounts FFm*	*Plans FFm*
1966	198		2,577	
1970	487	363	5,878	4,284
1975	928	2,925	12,184	44,920
1980	2,645	4,803	46,288	123,799
1981	3,008	4,864	53,638	130,906
1982	3,426	5,032	61,111	139,804
1983	3,787	5,726	66,001	156,785

Source: Ministry of Finance, *Les Notes Bleues* (various issues).

accounts and FF36.1 billion for plans. The plans are clearly far more popular than the accounts. The ratio of loans to deposits has risen sharply for the plans from nothing in 1973, to 12 per cent in 1977, 46 per cent in 1981 and 74 per cent in 1983. The ratio of loans to deposits for the accounts has fluctuated markedly, reaching a high point of 60 per cent in 1974 before falling, as a result of the popularity of the plans, to 40 per cent in 1979 and then rising to 59 per cent in 1983. These figures show the funding problem inherent in contract savings schemes. The number of new members has to be continually increased in order to meet commitments to existing members.

Unlike in West Germany there are no specialist institutions which offer the contract scheme only. The banks have about 78 per cent of the market, the savings banks 17 per cent and the National Savings Bank 5 per cent. Within the banking sector the Crédit Agricole is the market leader.

The Homeloan Scheme in Britain

The possibility of contractual savings schemes has been raised from time to time in Britain. In fact, some building societies and other lenders do offer guaranteed loan schemes, by which an individual is promised a loan after he has saved a certain amount. However, the terms of such schemes are identical to normal savings and borrowing, and generally they have had very little impact.

However, a government scheme was introduced as a result of the consultative paper on housing policy (DoE, 1977). The Green Paper outlined the basis of the scheme as being a government savings bonus up to a maximum of £100, and an interest-free loan of £500 for five years. In 1978 the government introduced the Homeloan Scheme, which differed only slightly from the Green Paper proposal. To qualify for the bonus a prospective first-time homebuyer must save for two years with a building society or other participating institution. One full year before applying for the bonus at least £300 must have been saved; throughout the year before applying for the bonus £300 must be kept in the account. If these conditions are satisfied the saver will qualify for the minimum bonus of £40. The bonus provision gradually increases according to the level of savings held and if £1,000 is held throughout the twelve-month period the maximum bonus of £110 is available.

The second part of the scheme involves a government loan of £600, which is available if £600 is in the savings account when the loan is applied for. The loan is interest free for the first five years that it is outstanding, and no capital repayments are required during this period.

Finally, the benefits are only available to first-time buyers purchasing houses within price limits defined for each region of the country. The limits are set with the intention of enabling approximately two-thirds of first-time buyers to obtain the benefits and are amended periodically.

At the time the scheme was introduced it was argued by the government that it would represent a major contribution towards assisting first-time buyers. The government's public expenditure White Paper published in January 1979 (two months after the introduction of the scheme) envisaged government expenditure of £58 million in 1980–1 (representing bonuses paid on savings and interest foregone on loans), rising to £103 million in 1981–2. However, within two years government provisions for expenditure on the scheme had fallen to less than £10 million. Table 6.4 shows the progress of the scheme.

Table 6.4 *The Homeloan Scheme*

Year	*Number of purchasers receiving assistance*	*Gross amount of assistance given* *£m*	*Loans repaid* *£m*
1981–2	5,545	3.87	0.03
1982–3	6,277	4.36	0.12
1983–4	4,420	2.95	0.47
1984–5	3,580	2.50	0.89

Source: HMSO, 1986.

During the period covered by the table building societies made loans to around 1.9 million first-time buyers, of which around 1.3 million (two-thirds) would have been eligible for assistance under the scheme. As the table shows, only about 20,000 people took advantage of the scheme and the total cost to the government was only a fraction of that envisaged.

In some respects the Homeloan Scheme is similar to those run in France and West Germany. It involves a period of saving before a loan becomes available, and the loan is available on preferential terms as a result of government subsidy. Nevertheless, it is fair to say that the scheme has been a complete failure. It is now almost totally ignored by lending institutions and there is little demand from first-time buyers.

The reasons for this failure are not difficult to appreciate. The Building Societies Association identified the major problem in its initial memorandum to societies on the subject, when it said that the scheme can 'hardly be characterised as straightforward'. The problem is that the benefits are minor (and indeed unchanged since 1978) compared to the complexity of the scheme. It has already been stressed that people in Britain buy their first homes at a relatively young age; few take the trouble to plan two years ahead, especially if the benefits of so doing are as small as those offered by the Homeloan Scheme. If contractual saving for house purchase is to have a future in Britain the scheme must be considerably simplified, or the benefits increased. Neither course seems likely to be adopted and it may be expected that the scheme will continue to wither gradually.

PART III

The British Housing Finance Market

7 Government Regulation and Support of the Housing Finance Market

Mortgage Law

A mortgage is a charge over property, conferred by the owner on a lender, in order to secure the repayment of a loan. In each of the United Kingdom's three legal jurisdictions (England and Wales, Northern Ireland, Scotland) the law of mortgages is old, technical and very complicated. The law in Northern Ireland shares the same historical roots as that in England and Wales but has developed separately. In Scotland, the law is quite different – and the term 'heritable security' is used rather than 'mortgage'. However, in all three jurisdictions the law is influenced by two basic principles.

The first is that the object of a mortgage is to secure a loan. If the borrower fails to repay the loan secured by the mortgage, or breaks the terms of the loan agreement in other ways, the lender can obtain possession of the property (that is, he can use the machinery of the courts to remove the owner from the property if he is still there), sell the property and repay the loan out of the proceeds. The law obliges him to sell the property for the best price he can reasonably get and, if this is more than what he is owed, to pay the surplus to other lenders who have mortgages over the property or to the borrower.

The second principle is that the borrower should not be treated unfairly by the lender. This principle manifests itself in various ways, but the most important is that the borrower can at any time discharge the mortgage by repaying the outstanding amount of the loan. Any provision in the mortgage which would prevent him from doing this (by 'clogging the equity of redemption', to use the legal term) is invalid.

This feature is particularly important in respect of loans at fixed rates of interest. As a matter of commercial prudence, a lender can safely make loans at fixed rates of interest only if the borrower is prevented from redeeming, unless he effectively compensates the lender for any loss which will be incurred to him through redemption of the loan. If a long-term loan is taken out at a rate of interest of, say, 20 per cent, and market rates fall to, say, 10 per cent, then a lender could not allow a borrower to redeem unless, in effect, twice the mortgage debt was repaid to compensate for the loss of interest which the lender would receive. This practice is followed in a number of other countries, for example, Denmark. However, in Britain, this would be ruled as a clog on the equity and would be unenforceable.

A typical housing finance loan agreement in Britain would, besides granting a security over the home to be purchased with the loan, also cover the following points:

(1) A promise by the borrower to repay the loan, either by monthly payment of capital and interest, or by monthly payments of interest only, with the debt being repaid at the end of the term out of the proceeds of an insurance policy.
(2) A promise by the borrower to do various other things, for example, to keep the property in good condition and not to let it without permission.
(3) Provisions concerning the rate of interest and how it can be varied.
(4) Usually, provisions about insuring the property (often the lender insures the property on behalf of both himself and the borrower).

The house purchase process is facilitated by a land registration system which now covers some 80 per cent of England and Wales. The Land Registry maintains details of the ownership of all registered land, and also details of charges against the land. This means that there is no necessity for the detailed title inquiries that are needed, for example, in America where there is not such a comprehensive land registration system. All that is necessary is for the appropriate inquiries to be made of the Land Registry, and for the change of ownership and changes in the charges on the property to be registered after completion. A similar system is being introduced in Scotland.

The Cost of House Purchase

House purchase in Britain is relatively cheap compared with other countries. Perhaps this partly reflects the fact that in Britain people move more frequently than in other countries, itself largely a consequence of the lack of rented accommodation. High taxes on the transfer of houses would not be as acceptable as they are in countries where people tend to purchase only one house.

Someone wishing to purchase a house normally first approaches an estate agent. The agents charge commission to those selling, and no charge is made to potential purchasers. An agent may either act as a sole agent, in which case his commission charge is lower, or a property may be put on the books of several agents, in which case a higher charge is made. Estate agency charges are generally between 1 per cent and 2 per cent of the purchase price. The estate agent undertakes to find a purchaser, and increasingly acts as a mortgage intermediary, but generally does little else in the house purchase process. The fee payable by the vendor to the estate agent is subject to value added tax (VAT) which at present is levied at the rate of 15 per cent.

The purchaser will have to meet legal fees incurred in transferring the ownership of the property to him. Traditionally, solicitors have had a monopoly of conveyancing in Britain, but this is changing. There is now provision for licensed conveyancers, the first of whom will be operating in 1987. The solicitors employed by lending institutions such as building societies are not allowed to undertake conveyancing work. There has been much criticism of conveyancing costs in the recent past, but recently competition in the market, and the threat of new entrants, has reduced fees substantially. Typical conveyancing costs are between 0.75 per cent and 1 per cent of the purchase price of the property, but can be lower. Where a property is to be mortgaged, the purchaser will normally have to pay the legal costs of the lender. Usually the lender will use the purchaser's solicitor with a resultant saving in costs. A typical fee for preparing the mortgage deed is about £100. VAT is levied on both the conveyancing charge and the charge for preparing the mortgage deed.

Stamp duty is levied on the purchase price of the property where it is in excess of £30,000. The rate of duty is currently 1 per cent on the whole of the purchase price, not just on the amount by which it exceeds £30,000. Stamp duty rates were reduced in the 1984 Budget, the duty previously having been levied at a maximum rate of 2 per cent.

The total costs facing the house buyer are therefore likely to be only 3 or 4 per cent of the house price, substantially less than in other countries.

Consumer Credit Legislation

Consumer credit generally in Britain is regulated under the Consumer Credit Act 1974. This was not aimed at housing finance, and indeed many of its provisions still do not apply to housing finance. The Act itself followed the Report of the Crowther Committee into Consumer Credit, which was published in 1971. The aim of the Act is to bring about protection for consumers obtaining credit, and also to replace a multitude of previous Acts of Parliament, all of which applied to credit. The main purposes of the Act are:

(1) To regulate the formation, terms and enforcement of credit and hire purchase agreements by conferring certain rights on consumers and placing restraints on the suppliers of credit.
(2) To set up a licensing system (administered by the Director General of Fair Trading) for those engaged in consumer credit business.
(3) To provide a common system for measuring interest rates.

(4) To control door-to-door canvassing to persuade consumers to apply for credit.
(5) To prevent undesirable methods of seeking credit business, such as misleading advertisements.
(6) To make it impossible to contract out of the provisions of the Act.
(7) To protect borrowers from gross and extortionate credit bargains.

However, the Act effectively excluded much of lending for housing purposes. All loans over £5,000 (recently raised to £15,000) were outside the Act, which also exempted all consumer credit agreements (whether for house purchase or not) secured on land, and made by a building society or local authority. There was no such exclusion for banks or other lenders, one indication of the different regulations applying to different participants in the market.

However, all lenders are now subject to the Advertisements and Quotations Regulations made under the Act. The government has also indicated that it intends to bring the treatment of banks and building societies into line by exempting their mortgage lending only where it is for house purchase or improvement. Thus, even where banks and societies make loans secured on first mortgage, these will not be exempted from the full provisions of the Act unless they are for house purchase or improvement.

The three regulations to which all lenders are now subject are the Total Charge for Credit Regulations, the Advertisements Regulations and the Quotations Regulations. Through the first of these regulations the concept of the rate of total charge for credit (commonly known as annual percentage rate or APR) is introduced. This takes account of all interest payments, initial charges and all other charges for a loan. It does not, however, take into account tax relief, life insurance premiums or any interest rate changes.

The Advertisements Regulations are intended to ensure that lenders make available comprehensive information about their terms, if they advertise. In a 'full credit advertisement' lenders must give their name and address, their security requirements, where applicable requirements as to life insurance, and financial information in the form of the APR, the total amount payable (TAP), the amount the lender is willing to lend, the amount of the repayments and the term.

The Quotations Regulations require that if a prospective borrower asks a lender for written information, then the lender must give a document which basically sets out the same information as a full credit advertisement.

In practice, the regulations have had little effect on the market. The demand from consumers for quotations under the regulations has been negligible. Advertisements for mortgage credit do now generally state a typical APR as well as the nominal rate of the lender, but most discussion in the press still refers only to nominal rates. There are a number of reasons for this. The first is that the difference between the APR and the nominal rate in the case of a long-term mortgage loan is relatively small, generally no more than one percentage point. By contrast, for short-term credit agreements, the difference can be huge, a flat rate of 10 per cent sometimes equating to an APR of 25 per cent. Perhaps more importantly, the APR can indicate only the mortgage rate at the time the loan is taken out. Given the variable rate nature of mortgages in the United Kingdom, this is of comparatively little use to the consumer because the quoted APR can be altered almost without notice by the lender. Shopping around cannot overcome this problem, because again it can only show which is the cheapest lender at a given point of time, rather than over the life of the loan.

However, the various regulations have forced all lenders to look more carefully at the method by which they charge interest. Building societies, for example, generally charge interest on an annual rest basis, by which interest payments due in the year are based on the amount of the loan outstanding at the beginning of the year. Moreover, no account is taken of the timing of the regular repayments. This could mean that one person could effectively be paying a significantly higher rate for his loan than another, purely because of the date on which they took out their respective loans and the date on which the first payment fell due. Lenders have therefore looked at their procedures again, and have tried to iron out these various anomalies, largely so as to be able to quote a lower APR for a given nominal rate. This is an example of legislation perhaps having an unintended but nevertheless beneficial effect, even if on the face of it the consumer credit legislation is hardly used at all in the housing finance market.

Generally, it can be said that the Consumer Credit Act 1974 does not have a significant effect on the operation of the market. Lenders have learned to live with it. The interest on the part of consumers in legislation designed to protect them is almost insignificant.

Legislation Applying to Specific Bodies

The various operators in the housing finance market are subject to differing legislation. Building societies are governed by specific building society legislation, the banks and insurance companies are subject to company law and also specific banking and insurance legislation respectively, and local authorities are subject to specific laws governing their operations. This section of the chapter considers special provisions applying to the various lenders.

In the case of building societies, this is somewhat difficult, as their legislation is undergoing a major change. Societies have operated under the Building Societies Act 1962 as amended, and statutory instruments under that and other acts. A new bill was considered by Parliament in the first six months of 1986, and this became the Building Societies Act 1986, coming into operation in 1987. This discussion is based on the new legislation rather than the 1962 Act.

Building societies will be subject to various limits on the proportion of their assets which they can hold in certain categories. The Act introduces the concept of commercial assets, which basically are total assets less fixed assets and liquid assets. Of total commercial assets, 90 per cent must be in the form of first mortgage loans on residential property to be occupied, broadly speaking, by the borrower. Within the remaining 10 per cent, not more than 5 per cent of commercial assets can be in unsecured loans or ownership of land and property. There is provision in the Act for the minimum percentage of assets which must be held in first mortgage loans (Class 1 assets) to be reduced to 75 per cent. However, it should be noted that there is no limit on building society lending for house purchase as such by virtue of these provisions. Rather, the limits are on the other activities of societies, and are designed to ensure that societies remain predominantly specialists in housing finance.

It is important to note that building societies can make Class 1 loans only if they have a first mortgage over the property, and if it is for the residential use of the owner. (There are certain exceptions designed to cover those living in tied accommodation, houses occupied by dependent relatives and part-owner-occupied properties.) It is not therefore open to building societies to make unsecured loans to finance owner-occupation within their Class 1 category.

Building societies must also comply with several other requirements in respect of their first mortgage loans. Particularly important is that they cannot make a mortgage loan conditional on the borrower using one of the various other services which societies are able to provide. They are also required to price each such service separately. Thus if a building society is providing a one-stop house buying service, it has to indicate separately any charge which it is making for conveyancing, the charge for surveying, and any charge for setting up the loan, as well as the rate of interest on the loan itself. Finally, building societies, unlike other institutions, are legally obliged to undertake a valuation of the property offered as security (although in practice most lenders follow this procedure).

Local authority lending is now at a very low level, and can largely be disregarded for the purposes of this book. In the early 1970s local authorities accounted for up to a quarter of new lending but the previous Labour and present Conservative governments have effectively prevented local authorities from making new loans for house purchase other than to finance sales of former council houses under the Right-to-Buy programme. The local authorities operate largely on a non-market basis. They are obliged, under the Housing Act 1980 (now consolidated into the Housing Act 1985), to charge a rate of interest that is the higher of the pooled cost of their funds or a rate stipulated by the Secretary of State for the Environment, which is invariably the typical building society rate. Under the Housing and Planning Act local authorities also have to obtain the specific consent of borrowers before mortgage loans can be transferred. A number of local authorities had begun to transfer their loans during 1985 as a means of raising additional capital, so avoiding government constraints on capital spending. The restrictions on sales were probably more aimed at curbing the raising of such money than influencing sales as such.

Banks are subject to no special legislation in respect of their mortgage lending. However, they are regulated as banks by the Bank of England and are, for example, subject to certain capital requirements. Significantly, mortgage lending is categorized as a relatively risky asset in terms of the risk asset classification used by the Bank of England. It stands alongside loans to any other sterling borrower, notwithstanding the high degree of security offered by British residential mortgage loans.

There are a number of other institutions in the housing finance market which are unregulated. Mortgage brokers, estate agents, solicitors and other intermediaries introduce business to building societies and other lenders, but they are subject to virtually no regulation. There has also been the emergence of four institutions, the National Home Loans Corporation, the Mortgage Funding Corporation, the Household Mortgage Corporation and the Mortgage Corporation, which raise their funds entirely on the wholesale markets, and operate by purchasing loans, as well as by making loans directly. Because the institutions are not deposit-taking bodies, they are not subject to regulation by the Bank of England.

It may well be the case within a few years that the evolving nature of the British mortgage market will require the government to consider whether there should be common rules applying to all lenders; that is, functional regulation rather than the present unsatisfactory regulation, or lack of it, by type of institution.

Tax Relief on Mortgage Interest

The main form of state support for owner-occupation in Britain is through tax relief on mortgage interest. As a policy issue, this is considered in Chapter 12. In this chapter, the rules governing tax relief are described, following which is a brief description of the implications of tax relief. It is first necessary to put tax relief in context.

Housing is both a consumption good and an investment good, the latter because it yields a stream of services over its life. There are therefore grounds for arguing that housing should be taxed as an investment good or as a consumption good, but clearly not both. If housing was to be taxed as an investment good, this would mean levying a tax on notional rental income (that is, the rent which owner-occupiers are assumed to receive from themselves), against which could be offset necessary expenditure such as interest costs and repairs and maintenance. In Britain, taxing of notional rental income was discontinued in 1963. However, tax relief on mortgage interest remains, and this can be regarded as a subsidy to the homebuyer, in that he is able to borrow to purchase housing at a lower rate than he can borrow to purchase other commodities.

In Britain, there is a local property tax in the form of rates, and this can be regarded as a tax on the value of a house and therefore it equates to a tax on notional rental income. However, rates are payable by all households, not just owner-occupiers. Also, there is a generous rate rebate scheme, through which low income households have a proportion of their rates, or even the whole of their rates, met through government subsidy. The present government intends that in the future all householders should pay at least 20 per cent of their rates and also has longer-term plans to abolish the rating system.

Finally, there is the question of capital gains taxation. This is a very complicated subject which cannot be discussed in detail here. Briefly, the position is that an owner-occupied house is exempt from capital gains tax. Depending on how one does the arithmetic, it might be seen that this yields a substantial subsidy. That is, if one assumes that on the sale of a house nominal profits should be subject to capital gains tax at 30 per cent, then it would seem that the cost of exemption is very high. In fact, such a calculation would not be valid. Capital gains tax has itself been index-linked, such that now only real capital gains are taxed. Moreover, there is roll-over relief through which tax can be deferred if the sale of one good coincides with the purchase of a similar one. More generally, it has proved fairly easy for people to avoid capital gains tax by ordering their financial affairs in an appropriate way.

In general it can be said that the investment aspect of the demand for house purchase has declined since 1980. This is partly because of the return of positive real interest rates, and also because of changes in capital gains tax, which have served to reduce the preferential position which housing previously enjoyed. More particularly, indexation of the tax generally has reduced its impact and hence the value of exemption from it.

Interest on a loan qualifies for tax relief where it is used either for purchasing a property, or for improving a property, or for paying off another loan which itself was for the purchase or improvement of the property. Relief is obtainable only where the property is the only or main residence of the borrower, his divorced or separated spouse or a dependent relative, or is to be used in this way within twelve months of the loan being made. Tax relief may also be obtained if the property is being purchased with a view to future occupation as a main residence by a borrower currently living in job-related accommodation.

The main restriction on tax relief is that it is available only on interest paid on that part of a loan up to £30,000. Tax relief in Britain is now granted through the MIRAS (Mortgage Interest Relief at Source) system, which was introduced in 1983. Basically, this system involves mortgage repayments being calculated after deduction of basic rate tax relief, with the government paying the lender an amount equivalent to this tax relief. For example, when the mortgage rate is 11 per cent and the basic rate of tax is 29 per cent, then repayments are calculated on the basis of a rate of 7.81 per cent (71 per cent of 11 per cent). The system is deliberately designed to ensure that even borrowers who would not be eligible for tax relief, because their income is so low, are able to obtain a corresponding benefit by paying a lower net of tax rate. It subsumed the Option Mortgage Scheme which previously catered for this group. Where a borrower pays tax at above the basic rate, then he is entitled to relief on his mortgage interest payments at his highest marginal rate. The basic rate element is given through the MIRAS system, with the higher rate element being given through tax coding, or in annual tax assessments. Until 1983 all relief, including that at the basic rate, was given through an individual's tax coding, which was increased by an amount equivalent to the interest paid.

The effective net of tax rate paid by various borrowers for different amounts of loan, both the marginal and the average rate, is illustrated in Table 7.1. This rather complicated matrix shows the very low cost of a relatively small mortgage, especially for higher rate taxpayers. For all borrowers there is a sharp rise in the marginal cost of a mortgage at £30,000, and the higher the rate of tax to which the borrower is subject the greater the jump. It needs to be noted here that basic rate taxpayers can obtain a higher return on an investment in a building society than the cost of their loan. For higher rate taxpayers, able to take advantage of tax-free national savings certificates and tax favoured index-linked and low coupon gilts, the gap between the net cost of a mortgage and net yield on an investment is substantial.

Table 7.1 *Average and Marginal Cost of a Mortgage at 11 Per Cent Nominal Rate*

Marginal	*£20,000*		*£30,000*		*£60,000*		*£80,000*	
rate of tax %	*Average cost %*	*Marginal cost %*	*Average cost %*	*Marginal cost %*	*Average cost %*	*Marginal cost %*	*Average cost %*	*Marginal cost %*
0	7.8	7.8	7.8	11.0	9.4	11.0	9.8	11.0
29	7.8	7.8	7.8	11.0	9.4	11.0	9.8	11.0
40	6.6	6.6	6.6	11.0	8.8	11.0	9.4	11.0
50	5.5	5.5	5.5	11.0	8.3	11.0	8.9	11.0
60	4.4	4.4	4.4	11.0	7.7	11.0	8.5	11.0

Parenthetically, it may be wondered how building societies are able to undertake their business in a profitable manner in the light of the statement above that basic rate taxpayers can obtain a higher return on their investment with a building society than their loan with the building society costs. This is a temporary phenomenon caused by the existence of a substantial, but rapidly diminishing, tranche of investors' funds held at well below market rates of interest in ordinary shares. The low rates of interest paid on these balances enable building societies to pay rates on their other accounts that are greater than the income generated by the mortgages which they fund. As the level of transfers between accounts within building societies has accelerated, the proportion of balances in ordinary shares has declined so that by the end of 1985 less than 20 per cent of all funds held were in this category. Fairly soon the balances will be so small that they will no longer provide a cushion to the higher rated accounts and the arbitraging possibilities of borrowing from a building society and re-investing the proceeds in the same society will disappear.

This picture suggests that it makes sense for any house purchaser to have a mortgage loan up to £30,000 and for higher rate taxpayers the benefit is very substantial. However, as noted earlier, at £30,000 there is a sharp increase in the marginal cost of a mortgage and the borrower has to decide whether the notional rate of return on the house exceeds the mortgage rate or whether he can obtain a higher return than the cost of the mortgage on an alternative investment.

It is inevitable that this situation feeds through to the mortgage and housing markets, affecting the nominal mortgage rate and the level of house prices. These points are considered in more detail in Chapter 12, and at this stage it is sufficient to say that tax relief on mortgage interest is probably the single most important variable influencing the behaviour of the mortgage market.

Supplementary Benefit for Mortgage Interest

A second important feature of the housing finance market is government support for borrowers who are unable to maintain their mortgage interest. This is achieved through one of many state benefits, supplementary benefit, which is available to people who are not in full-time employment and who do not otherwise have enough money to live on. Weekly payments are made to bring income up to a standard at which it should be possible to make ends meet. The claimant's requirements are made up of a weekly living allowance, together with housing costs and additional requirements which a claimant can prove. For owner-occupiers, mortgage interest payments will be met in full, unless they are considered to be unreasonable. An allowance of £1.85 a week for repairs and insurance is also paid, and in addition the benefit covers water rates and any ground rent or service charges. Benefit does not, however, cover the capital part of mortgage repayments. Benefit is not paid if a claimant or his partner has savings in excess of £3,000.

Supplementary benefit is of great importance in enhancing the security of

Table 7.2 *Mortgage Arrears and Possessions, Building Societies, 1979–85*

Period	*No. of loans at end of period*	*Properties taken into possession in period*		*Loans 6–12 months in arrear, end period*		*Loans over 12 months in arrear, end period*	
		No.	*%*	*No.*	*%*	*No.*	*%*
1979	5,264,000	2,530	0.048	8,420	0.16		
1980	5,396,000	3,020	0.056	13,490	0.25		
1981	5,505,000	4,240	0.077	18,720	0.34		
1982	5,664,000	5,950	0.105	23,790	0.42	4,810	0.085
1983	5,949,000	7,320	0.123	25,580	0.43	6,540	0.11
1984	6,354,000	10,870	0.171	41,940	0.66	8,260	0.13
1985	6,636,000	16,590	0.250	49,110	0.74	11,280	0.17
1981 H1	5,475,000	1,810	0.033	15,880	0.29		
H2	5,505,000	2,420	0.044	18,720	0.34		
1982 H1	5,570,000	2,670	0.048	20,610	0.37	3,230	0.058
H2	5,664,000	3,290	0.058	23,790	0.42	4,810	0.085
1983 H1	5,746,000	3,390	0.059	27,010	0.47	6,900	0.12
H2	5,949,000	3,930	0.066	25,580	0.43	6,540	0.11
1984 H1	6,129,000	5,210	0.085	28,810	0.47	7,970	0.13
H2	6,354,000	5,660	0.089	41,940	0.66	8,260	0.13
1985 H1	6,460,000	7,300	0.113	43,280	0.67	9,040	0.14
H2	6,636,000	9,290	0.140	49,110	0.74	11,280	0.17

Source: The Building Societies Association (1986b).

Notes:

1 The figures are based on statistics provided by some or all of the fifteen largest societies which accounted for 85 per cent of all outstanding mortgages at the end of 1985. The figures have been grossed up to represent the whole industry by reference to the number of outstanding mortgage loans as published by the Chief Registrar of Friendly Societies. The figures for 1985 are BSA estimates. (It should be noted that the figures refer to the number of mortgage loans and not to the number of borrowers.)

2 The figures have been rounded to the nearest 10 to avoid a spurious impression of accuracy.

3 H1 refers to first half of calendar year; H2 refers to second half of calendar year.

4 The figures for possessions are based on a sample of eleven societies up to the end of 1981 and there is therefore a slight discontinuity in the series at this time.

5 Properties taken into possession include those voluntarily surrendered.

6 Properties in possession are not also counted as loans in arrear.

7 The figures for loans 6–12 months in arrear prior to the end of 1982 should be treated with considerable caution.

8 MIRAS and reductions in the mortgage rate have had the effect of reducing monthly repayments and hence increasing the number of months in arrear which a given amount represents. The figures for arrears cannot be used to show precise trends over time.

mortgage lending. In the normal course of events, one would expect unemployment to lead to mortgage default and repossession by the lender. In areas of high unemployment, the cumulative effects of a number of such cases could be to depress house prices, thus further jeopardizing the security of lenders. In Britain, however, the payment of supplementary benefit helps to prevent these developments from occurring, and effectively underpins the housing finance market.

During the summer of 1985 the government announced that it would be considering ways of reducing the cost to public funds of this form of benefit, and in May 1986 it announced a proposal that benefit would be available to cover only half of the mortgage interest payable for the first six months of unemployment. It is uncertain what effect this would have on the housing finance market; it seems likely, however, that lenders would become more reluctant to make high percentage advances to borrowers believed to have a high chance of becoming unemployed.

Arrears and Mortgage Losses

It is apparent that mortgage lending is an extremely secure form of lending in Britain. Tax relief on mortgage interest effectively reduces the cost of mortgage loan finance by a considerable amount, and supplementary benefit provides valuable support where borrowers become unemployed. Moreover, for most of the recent past, the mortgage market has been undersupplied with funds, as a result of which lenders have not had to take great risks. The overall result is that mortgage losses and arrears are extremely low. In 1984, building societies recorded mortgage losses of just £4 million on a portfolio of £80 billion, and their provision for losses at the end of the year was just £5 million. These figures are about 0.5 per cent of the losses reported by the major British clearing banks on the full range of their business.

Mortgage arrears and possessions also remain extremely low in relation to the volume of business undertaken by building societies. However, there has been a sharp upward trend in the past few years, reflecting the high and rising level of unemployment. Estimated figures for possessions and arrears of the whole industry are shown in Table 7.2.

8 Loan Terms and Instruments

In any housing finance system a lending institution must have a set of rules, or at least basic criteria, to enable it to decide what types of property it wishes to accept as security for its loans, which individuals it will lend to, how much it will lend to them, and what interest rate it will charge. Such criteria will not usually be absolute. They will change over time according to the availability of funds for lending, the state of the economy and especially the level of interest rates, the level of government support for, or intervention in, the mortgage market, and the amount of competition for new business. What is regarded as bad lending practice one year can become the accepted procedure the next.

Lending criteria are essential not only to guide the lender. The borrower will also need to know the terms and conditions on which he can obtain a loan. In Britain in the 1960s and 1970s lending terms were often unpublicized as the lending institutions were unable to meet the demand for mortgages and did not need to advertise their services. Borrowers generally had no choice but to accept the terms they were offered. In the mid-1980s the increasingly competitive mortgage market has led to more widespread advertising of mortgages, and a greater degree of innovation so that borrowers are now able to compare the differing terms available and choose the package most suitable to their needs.

Lending Criteria

Most loans for house purchase are secured on the property that is being bought. This means that if the borrower fails to maintain the agreed level of repayments the lender is able, under the terms of the mortgage contract, to take possession of the property and sell it in order to realize the outstanding loan. The most important features of the property, therefore, from the lender's point of view, are its value, especially in relation to the size of the advance, and its marketability. As we have seen, British building societies have, by law, to obtain a valuation report from a qualified person before they are able to make an advance, and other lenders will also normally go through this procedure. The valuation is a fairly superficial examination giving the lender basic information on the property.

Generally, the value ascribed to the dwelling will be close to, or the same as, the price agreed by the vendor and purchaser. There are, however, exceptions. Between 1979 and 1985 over 750,000 council houses were sold to sitting tenants at significant discounts to their free market price, and in these cases the valuation was always above the price. At the opposite extreme some new houses built in the early 1980s were valued below their free market price because a significant proportion of that price reflected the large number of consumer durables (such as refrigerators, ovens and carpets) built into the property which, unlike the house itself, could be expected to decline in value fairly rapidly, thus reducing the security enjoyed by the lender. In any case, building societies can, by law, lend only on the security of the property itself.

Most lenders are unable or are reluctant to lend on certain types of property. In the case of building societies part of such a restriction is imposed by law; it is not possible for a society to lend on the security of a house boat. More generally, lenders will often require property in a poor state of repair to be improved before they will provide funds. There are also a few examples of structurally sound types of property which most lenders will tend to avoid.

The first of these is short-leasehold flats. Most flats in Britain are leasehold; that is, the owner purchases the right to live in the flat for a certain period, often ninety-nine years, after which time the ownership of the flat reverts to the freeholder. The freeholder owns the land on which the flats are built and is responsible for the upkeep of the common parts of the building, such as gardens, staircases, external walls and so on. In return for this maintenance each leaseholder will pay a ground rent to the freeholder, and a service charge. Near the beginning of a lease the property will be very marketable, and the same will apply when there are eighty, seventy or sixty years remaining. Where there are only twenty-five years remaining marketability tends to become more of a problem. Few people will wish to purchase a property with the help of a mortgage loan, pay off that loan over twenty-five years and then find that they have nothing to show for their expenditure. The amount that any individual will be prepared to pay for a flat near the end of its lease will gradually decline as the full term approaches and so lenders have diminishing security for their loans. Most lenders therefore stipulate that a lease must have at least twice as many years to run as the mortgage term.

A rather different problem faces the lender in assessing the value of, and security offered by, freehold flats. In this case ownership passes from purchaser to purchaser in perpetuity, but often there are inadequate arrangements regarding the upkeep of the common parts of the property, and this can result in a gradual decline in the appearance and, more importantly, the structural soundness of the property. Again, many lenders are reluctant to make advances on this type of security.

In the past it has been alleged that some lenders have refused to lend on certain properties not because of their tenure or state of repair, but because of the area in which they are located. Thus in the early 1970s building societies were accused of 'red-lining' certain inner-city areas, that is, drawing a line on a map around areas in which they were not willing to lend, whatever the status or condition of the property. Such allegations were never satisfactorily proved, but there is no doubt that some lenders used to refuse to lend on property built before 1919 on the grounds that such property was reaching the end of its useful life and did not provide adequate security for a long-term loan. Such attitudes tended to develop during the 1950s and 1960s when demolition, slum clearance and new building was the accepted way to improve the quality of the housing stock. By the mid-1970s attitudes had changed; rehabilitation of existing property was seen as a more rewarding use of resources, and an appreciation of the qualities of the older housing stock developed. At about this time building societies became more closely involved with the housing departments of local authorities and societies' attitude to older dwellings altered, in line with the more general change of attitudes. Between 1970 and 1980 the proportion of societies' new loans secured on pre-1919 dwellings rose from 17 per cent to 28 per cent, and red-lining allegations became less frequent.

While lenders are concerned with the marketability of the properties offered to them as security it also needs to be recognized that lenders' policy on certain types of property can affect their marketability. There is a two-way causality between marketability and lending practice. It is also the case that lenders owe a duty, morally if not legally, to potential borrowers, who may wish to purchase a property which will not in the long run represent a good investment, or provide adequate shelter. Such issues were raised in the early 1980s when it became clear that certain properties, built by unconventional methods involving the use of pre-reinforced concrete (p.r.c.), were likely to deteriorate fairly quickly. Most such properties were in the public sector, but a number had been sold to sitting tenants. As soon as the defects were discovered most lenders regarded the properties as offering inadequate security and also felt they had a duty to advise potential borrowers not to purchase them. Such a policy decision immediately affected the marketability of all dwellings involving p.r.c. construction methods, even where no sign of deterioration had been discovered, and left those living in such properties in a difficult position if they wished to sell. By the mid-1980s approved methods of repair were beginning to emerge and the marketability and mortgageability of improved dwellings increased.

Having valued the property a lender will need to decide what proportion of that value it is prepared to lend. In the past loans covering 100 per cent of the purchase price were regarded as bad lending practice. In circumstances where the purchaser is not required to make any contribution towards the purchase price lenders believed that the personal commitment of the borrower to repaying the loan was reduced. Also, the risks faced by a lender if house prices in general decline or rise only slowly, or if special factors reduce the value of an individual property, are greater if a large percentage of the value is lent. In theory lenders should be willing to lend greater percentages of the purchase price in times of rapid house price inflation, as high percentage loans are quickly transformed into low percentage loans. In fact, in Britain lending terms have become more liberal in the 1980s, at a time of moderately low inflation, because of competition to lend funds. During the rapid inflation of the 1970s relatively low percentage advances were imposed by lenders because the supply of funds to lend fell short of demand, and rationing devices were required.

In order to reduce the risks of high percentage advances most lenders require borrowers in this category to take out a mortgage indemnity policy. This reduces the lenders' risk of loss if the borrower defaults and the price obtained for the property following possession is not sufficient to pay off the loan and the lender's expenses. Most lenders in Britain require such a policy if the loan exceeds 70–80 per cent of the valuation.

Although the property is the security for the loan most lenders would not expect to take possession in order to obtain repayment of their loan. Rather, the loan, with interest, will be repaid in monthly instalments from the borrower's income. An assessment of this is an important part of a lender's pre-loan investigations. Generally, in Britain the maximum loan allowed will be expressed as a multiple of the applicant's income. This multiple tends to vary according to the availability of funds and the degree of competition in the mortgage market. In times of shortage lenders have restricted their maximum loans to 2.25 times income, but by the mid-1980s 2.75 or 3 times were commonly quoted maxima.

A lender will also be concerned with the applicant's supplementary income. Some lenders will take into account overtime earnings if these are regular, although clearly there is a risk of these disappearing during the period of the loan. Most lenders will also lend an amount equal to the second income of the household. Often, for a young married couple, this is the woman's income, which the lender might well expect to see disappear for a while, when the couple begin to raise children.

Most loans are scheduled for repayment over a term of twenty-five years, although borrowers can generally choose whichever term gives them a convenient profile of repayments. Some borrowers, especially those well into middle age, may choose a twenty-year term and some lenders ask that repayments be scheduled for completion before retirement, although this restriction is gradually disappearing. Younger borrowers may be able to choose a term of thirty or even thirty-five years, in order to reduce slightly the early repayments, but this is unusual. Most mortgages do not run their full term because borrowers move house and obtain a new mortgage, while those who stay in the same dwelling find that inflation so reduces the value of the debt in real terms that they are able to accelerate their repayments, or complete the repayments with a lump sum.

The terms on which premature redemption can be made are always covered in the mortgage deed, although the arrangements are rather less important under the British system of variable interest rates than under systems that use fixed rates of interest, a point discussed in more detail below. In Britain there are generally no charges for early redemption, although a few years ago some building societies made a charge of three months' interest if redemption took place within five years of the loan being granted and another loan was not taken out, arguing that the profit made on the loan in that short period was not sufficient to cover the costs of setting up the loan. Other lenders, mostly banks, have overcome this by charging an administrative fee at the time of application.

Types of Loan

Every mortgage deed commits the borrower to making regular payments, usually over twenty-five years, to the lender. Until 1983 the vast majority of loans were annuity, or repayment, loans which involved the borrower making monthly repayments of capital and interest. Since 1983 the majority of loans have been written on the endowment basis, which means that borrowers repay only interest to the lender, while simultaneously making regular contributions to an endowment insurance policy designed to mature at the end of the term of the mortgage loan, thus repaying the outstanding debt.

The annuity mortgage involves a series of constant repayments (assuming there is no change in the rate of interest applied to the loan). In the first year of the repayment term the bulk of the payments are interest and only a little capital is repaid. In the second year interest payments will be slightly less, because a small amount of capital has been paid off in the first year, and capital repayments are slightly higher, within the fixed repayment. Gradually the proportion of capital payments rises so that in the second half of the twenty-five year term, the bulk of the repayments are capital. The higher the interest rate, the smaller the initial proportion of capital in the repayments. As interest rates fall so the level and proportion of capital repayments in the early years of the loan rise.

Table 8.1 shows the split between payments of interest and capital for a £25,000 mortgage repayable over twenty-five years. It can be seen that in the first year 85 per cent of the total payment is interest and only a relatively small proportion of capital is paid off. It is not until year 17 that capital repayments exceed interest and not until year 18 that half the loan has been repaid.

The endowment mortgage is easier to understand in that the interest repayments remain constant throughout the term as long as the interest rates are not changed, because there are no capital repayments. The insurance premiums are also constant. Borrowers can take out a low-cost endowment policy which means that the sum assured will be only just sufficient to pay off the mortgage debt at maturity, or a full-cost policy which will give the

Table 8.1 *Advance of £25,000 Repayable Over Twenty-Five Years at 11 Per Cent (7.81 Per Cent with Mortgage Interest Relief at Source)*

Year	*Constant net annual repayment* £	*Principal* £	*Interest* £	*Balance end year* £
1	2,313.00	350.50	1,962.50	24,649.50
2	2,313.00	378.01	1,934.99	24,271.49
3	2,313.00	407.69	1,905.32	23,863.82
4	2,313.00	439.69	1,873,31	23,424.12
5	2,313.00	474.21	1,838.79	22,949.91
6	2,313.00	511.43	1,801.57	22,438.48
7	2,313.00	551.58	1,761.42	21,886.90
8	2,313.00	594.88	1,718.12	21,292.02
9	2,313.00	641.58	1,671.42	20,650.44
10	2,313.00	691.94	1,621.06	19,958.50
11	2,313.00	746.26	1,566.74	19,212.24
12	2,313.00	804.84	1,508.16	18,407.40
13	2,313.00	868.02	1,444.98	17,539.38
14	2,313.00	936.16	1,376.84	16,603.22
15	2,313.00	1,009.65	1,303.35	15,593.57
16	2,313.00	1,088.91	1,224.09	14,504.67
17	2,313.00	1,174.38	1,138.62	13,330.28
18	2,313.00	1,266.57	1,046.43	12,063.71
19	2,313.00	1,366.00	947.00	10,697.71
20	2,313.00	1,473.23	839.77	9,224.48
21	2,313.00	1,588.88	724.12	7,635.60
22	2,313.00	1,713.61	599.39	5,921.99
23	2,313.00	1,848.12	464.88	4,073.87
24	2,313.00	1,993.20	319.80	2,080.67
25	2,244.00	2,080.67	163.33	0
Total	57,756.00	25,000.00	32,756.00	

Notes:

1 Calculations assume annual rests and no changes in the interest rate.

2 Calculations allow for basic rate tax relief of 29 per cent.

borrower a significant lump sum, over and above that necessary to repay the loan. The endowment policy will also include an element of life assurance to repay the loan in the event of death. If they need life assurance annuity borrowers must effect a separate policy.

Mortgage interest payments are eligible for tax relief at the borrower's marginal tax rate. Until 1984 life assurance premiums also enjoyed tax relief, at 17.5 per cent, and this tended to attract some borrowers to this form of repayment. A major boost to sales of endowment-linked mortgages occurred in 1983 following the introduction of mortgage interest relief at source

(MIRAS). Before the introduction of MIRAS, borrowers had obtained tax relief through the Pay As You Earn (PAYE) coding system. From April 1983 the tax relief was paid directly to lenders, who thus, in effect, charged a lower interest rate to their borrowers. As noted earlier, a lower interest rate increases the repayments of capital in the early years of an annuity mortgage, and thus counteracts to some extent the effect of the reduced interest rate. There is, however, no similar effect on endowment mortgages, which reflect fully the interest rate reduction. Following the introduction of MIRAS there was therefore a large increase in the demand for endowment loans, and the proportion of all building society loans written on this basis rose from about 20 per cent to 66 per cent. The removal of life insurance premium relief the following year resulted in the proportion declining to around 55 per cent.

Monthly repayments under the two types of system are now broadly similar, but each has its advantages and disadvantages. The endowment mortgage offers the possibility of a lump sum at the end of the term, even after the debt has been repaid, and by maximizing interest payments throughout the repayment period also maximizes tax relief. It is, however, relatively inflexible. The annuity mortgage repayment term can be lengthened or shortened as the circumstances of the borrower change, or indeed interest payments only can be made for a while. None of these options is normally available under the endowment method. The final decision is usually the result of personal preferences, but because an insurance company will pay commission to lenders introducing endowment business, this type of loan is sometimes marketed more intensively.

Recently a third type of loan, basically a variant of the endowment mortgage, has appeared. Like endowment loans, pension mortgages involve the borrower making interest-only payments to the lender, but here simultaneously contributing to a pension scheme. On retirement part of the lump sum pension payment is used to repay the mortgage. The advantage of this scheme is that not only the interest payments are tax deductable at the borrower's marginal tax rate, but so also are the pension contributions. The disadvantage is that the scheme is really only suitable for the self-employed, while the drawback for the lender is that pension schemes, unlike insurance policies, cannot be assigned to the lender, thus increasing the lender's risk.

Interest Rates

So far this chapter has hardly mentioned the central condition, or term, of a mortgage contract, the rate of interest payable on the capital borrowed. In general terms, in Britain, the interest rate charged will vary over the term of loan and will reflect the overall level of interest rates in the economy. During the 1970s mortgage rates tended to be lower than other rates, partly because lenders and the governments of the day felt it necessary to protect existing borrowers from the full effects of an historically high general level of rates. Mortgage finance was thus cheaper than other forms of credit, leading to an increase in demand, without the necessary supply, as lenders offering low mortgage rates were unable to pay the high rates to savers that were necessary to attract the inflow of funds necessary to meet that demand.

In this situation it became general practice for building societies to establish a base lending rate for small loans and to charge a higher rate for larger loans. In economic terms this practice was difficult to defend. It was argued that those borrowers wishing to obtain a greater share of a scarce resource should pay for the privilege, but this ignored regional differences in house prices and loan requirements and also the fact that the expenses of administering one large loan are lower than those of five smaller loans each one-fifth the size. The practice of charging differential rates related to the size of the mortgage was attacked by the commercial banks when they entered the market in the early 1980s and was finally ended by most building societies in 1985.

It had also been the practice of most lenders to charge a higher rate of interest for endowment-linked loans than for annuity mortgages. The differential was supposed to compensate for the fact that the lender had to wait until the end of the mortgage term before obtaining the use of the capital to lend again to other house buyers. The argument may have had some force in the 1970s when it was in the interests of building societies to encourage repayment of capital as rapidly as possible so that the funds thus obtained could be re-lent to those in the mortgage queue. By the mid-1980s many lenders were looking for lending opportunities and did not want the problem of re-lending regular capital repayments. In these circumstances it was sensible to remove the penalty applying to endowment loans and most major lenders abolished this early in 1986.

Some building societies continue to charge various risk-related differentials, involving higher rates for properties of unusual construction, for high income multiples or for high percentage advances. These were more defensible than size-related differentials, but were nevertheless adopted by only a small minority of lenders. By the mid-1980s most lenders had a single mortgage rate for all classes of borrower.

The Variable Rate Loan

One of the major features of the British housing finance system is that the rate of interest charged on a mortgage loan can be changed during the term of the loan at the discretion of the lender without any legal restraint. Thus, anyone taking out a loan in May 1978 at 8.5 per cent would have been required to pay 15 per cent by January 1980, whereas in most other countries anyone borrowing initially at 8.5 per cent would expect to pay that rate throughout the entire period of their mortgage contract.

The British system can be criticized for exposing borrowers to large and unforeseeable swings in their mortgage repayments. However, it is probably the case that the British system has stood up to the shocks imposed by high inflation and interest rates rather better than other systems. The first advantage of the variable rate mortgage is that it ensures equality between borrowers. No matter when the mortgage was obtained, exactly the same interest rate will be paid. In the fixed rate system timing is crucial, and with rapidly fluctuating interest rates a borrower can commit himself to paying 10 per cent a year for twenty-five years only to find that six months later interest rates have fallen to, say, 7.5 per cent. The natural reaction of most borrowers to such a development would be to redeem their old mortgage and take on one at the new lower rate. However, this would place the lending institution in a very difficult situation in that it would have committed itself to paying the higher interest rate on its liabilities for the full term, and would be unable to re-invest the proceeds of redemptions at a rate sufficient to cover its fixed interest costs. A second characteristic of fixed rate systems therefore is that the borrower is 'locked-in' to his original lending institution (which is unlikely to allow redemptions except on very onerous terms) to a much greater extent than with the variable rate system.

A third advantage of the variable rate system is that interest rate movements have a much smaller effect on housing and mortgage market activity than in the fixed rate system. Under the latter arrangement if interest rates are perceived as being high few people will wish to borrow. Those with houses may need to reduce the price quite considerably in order to achieve a sale, so that it is likely that house price movements will be strongly correlated with interest rate changes to an extent unknown in Britain. Housebuilding and mortgage lending activity are also likely to be more variable than if existing mortgage rates are allowed to change. With the variable rate mortgage market reactions to changes in interest rates are likely to be muted; borrowers know that if they borrow at times of extremely high or low rates no long-term disadvantage or advantage is likely to accrue. The timing of the borrowing is therefore of little relevance.

One consequence of this is that governments find it more difficult to control economic activity in general and housing market activity in particular in an economy where variable rate loans are normal. Thus if the government feels that the housing market is overheating, a decision to raise rates is likely to have a smaller effect the more variable the mortgage rates are. Whether this should be regarded as an advantage or disadvantage of variable rates is difficult to decide. Some may welcome the relative impotence of governments to influence markets; others fear that governments are driven to more extreme interest rate policies in order to obtain a given effect on the market.

The final advantage of the variable rate system is that it is associated with healthier financial institutions. As noted earlier, high interest rates in fixed rate systems lead to depressions in house prices, thus endangering the lender's security on existing loans. This is likely to mean that only lower percentage advances are available, or that the costs of insurance of higher percentage advances are increased.

The fixed rate mortgage has also been associated with the financial problems faced by the savings and loan associations (S&Ls) in America. Throughout their history S&Ls had accepted deposits at variable rates (although within a maximum specified by the federal government), but granted loans at fixed rates. This system worked well while interest rates were stable. However, as rates gradually rose and as federal government controls on interest rates were gradually removed the S&Ls found themselves in an increasingly difficult position. In order to retain their short-term savings balances the associations were forced to increase the rates they paid to depositors. They could not, however, change the rates on the fixed term loans outstanding. In the early 1980s the so-called 'earnings crisis' forced many S&Ls into bankruptcy, severely disrupting the housing market and the wider financial markets.

As the variable rate mortgage has gained worldwide acceptance so there has been increased interest in overcoming its one inherent disadvantage – the problem of rapidly fluctuating payments. In Britain building societies have experimented with various ways of limiting the impact of rate changes. Some societies change the payments required of the borrower just once a year, while continuing to charge the actual rate to the account. The annual review of payments takes account of changes in the rate during the previous year in establishing the level of payments for the succeeding year. A number of lenders will extend the term of the mortgage in order to reduce repayments if the borrower requests this, although at high interest rates there is little benefit in extending the term beyond twenty-five years. Some lenders will also accept interest-only payments for a period if borrowers are in particular difficulties. Finally, it may be possible to capitalize the interest, that is, to add it on to the existing loan, for a short period, especially if the loan is small in relation to the value of the dwelling. It should be stressed that, despite these alternatives, the vast majority of borrowers pay increased interest rates as and when required.

Other countries, and especially those without a long experience of variable rates, have tended to overcome the problem by imposing restrictions on the extent to which institutions can vary rates. Some adjustable rate loans contracts in America have clauses restricting the rate change to no more than, say, one percentage point in a single year and five points over the life of the loan. Another way to protect the borrower is to impose notice restrictions so that the institution can change the rate only after, say, three months' notice has been given. In fact, British building societies used to operate under this constraint. Both of these 'remedies' have the effect of giving variable rate loans more of the characteristics of fixed rate loans, so that the problems associated with the fixed rate system become more apparent the more this type of protection is given to the borrower.

An alternative is to link the mortgage rate to some index of interest rates outside the control of the lender. One of the fears in those countries moving to a variable rate system is that institutions granted the power to change the price of a product after it has been purchased will use this power irresponsibly. In fact, this has not been the case in Britain, although increasing attention has been drawn to the practice of some lenders of charging higher rates to existing borrowers (who face certain costs in moving to other lenders even in a variable rate system) than to new borrowers, whom the institution is keen to attract. The best protection for existing borrowers is probably a clause in the mortgage deed preventing the lender from holding the rate of interest for existing borrowers above that for new borrowers. As there is now competition for new borrowers such rules ensure that institutions that hold their rates at an unreasonably high level will have difficulty in obtaining new business.

Low Start Repayment Patterns

In general terms conventional mortgage repayment packages involve a fairly heavy commitment at the beginning of the repayment period, but one that falls during the life of the loan according to the rate of increase of the borrower's income. Thus, if a borrower's income rises by 10 per cent a year the proportion of this income devoted to mortgage payments will halve in seven years, assuming that interest rates have not changed and tax considerations are ignored. Some borrowers may well favour packages where the highest real repayment is at the start of the term. Young married couples, for example, might wish to have high repayments initially, with a decline thereafter coinciding with the decision of the woman to give up work to have children. For other potential borrowers, however, incomes will be so low that a very high proportion will be taken by mortgage payments in the early years of the repayment term, leaving insufficient income to cover other essentials. In order to help such borrowers a number of low-start packages have been devised by lenders. These vary in their complexity but normally do not reduce the overall costs of purchasing a house, but rather impose a different time profile of repayments, reducing the payments at the beginning of the term, at the cost of some future penalty.

The simplest scheme merely involves the borrower making payments on a lower than standard mortgage rate in the early years of the loan, with the unpaid interest being added to the loan outstanding for later repayment. This method is helpful only where a fairly low percentage advance has been made, otherwise the loan outstanding will soon rise above the value of the security, and is therefore of little help to first-time buyers, who typically have a high percentage advance. A variant of this method has been used by some building societies in which the payments in the first two or three years are topped up by contributions from a savings account established by the borrower before taking out the loan. Another variant is provided by some insurance companies which allow the borrower to pay fairly modest premiums on the endowment policy in the early years in return for higher premiums later.

A number of more ambitious schemes have been introduced in the 1980s. The most popular (although still very small compared to the number of conventional mortgages written) is shared ownership. This involves the purchaser buying only a small proportion of the house, typically 25 per cent, and renting the remainder. In some circumstances it is possible to envisage the same institution providing the mortgage and owning the rented part of the property, with the borrower/tenant making one combined payment. Typically, however, it is a building society making the loan on these schemes, and as societies have not been allowed to own land (except their own offices) a second institution, either a local authority or housing association, is usually involved in the renting side of the agreement.

The shared ownership arrangement is not usually regarded as permanent. Generally there will be a 'staircasing' procedure whereby the individual can purchase additional shares in the property as and when they can be afforded. A purchaser/tenant initially buying 25 per cent of the property would probably expect to buy, with the help of mortgage finance, a further 25 per cent every two years, becoming the outright owner six years after moving into the property. Clearly, detailed arrangements must be made for the funding of repairs when a single property has two owners.

Equity mortgages work on the same general principle, but under rather different arrangements. In this case the lender will provide a mortgage at a much lower rate of interest than normal, in return for a proportion of the profit the borrower makes when selling the property. The legal arrangements involved with this type of deal can be very complex. They need to make provision, for example, for the effect of increases in value resulting from improvement work undertaken by the borrower, but not financed by the lender, the terms under which the property should be sold, and the arrangements for the maintenance of the dwelling. Some lenders may also wish to avoid this type of contract because they have no control over the timing of the sale of the house, which could be anything from one to fifty years after the initial purchase. The timing of the sale within the house price cycle will also be of concern to the lender, but not necessarily to the borrower, if he is purchasing another dwelling. The scope for argument and disagreement between borrower and lender is probably greater under the equity mortgage arrangement than under any other.

Another attempt to overcome the problems of high initial repayments is found in the concept of index-linked mortgages. Again, the lender provides finance at below the market rate of interest, in this case typically 3 or 4 per cent. Repayments are made as with a normal annuity mortgage, but at the end of each year the debt outstanding is revalued according to the growth of some indicator of general price levels – in Britain normally the Retail Price Index (RPI). In the early years of the mortgage the debt outstanding will normally increase because the debt-increasing effect of index linking will be greater than the debt-reducing effect of fairly small capital repayments. In later years the greater proportion of repayment will be capital, so that the mortgage is paid off in the normal way after twenty-five years.

This type of contract can be attractive to institutions, which are able to guarantee a real rate of return on their investment and therefore can offer similar contracts to savers or wholesale investors. The contract is, perhaps, not so attractive to the borrower, who needs to be fairly certain that his income will rise in line with retail prices over a fairly long period. A borrower obtaining only a 15 per cent pay increase in a year of 25 per cent price inflation could easily find his repayments spiralling out of control. In fact, these arrangements have so far been used in Britain only for the provision of rented housing. In one recent example a building society made index-linked funds available to a new town development corporation to build rented housing. Here there is a reasonable expectation that rents will rise in line with inflation, but no link between what any individual tenant pays and the RPI.

All of these arrangements are designed to allow those with low incomes to become owner-occupiers. There are dangers in this policy. The mortgage repayments are not the only costs of owner-occupation and it may be a mistake to concentrate on these to the exclusion of the costs of repairs, maintenance, decoration and rates which can often be equally damaging to the budgets of low-income families. Nevertheless, as long as applicants are properly screened by institutions, the arrangements described above can be a useful way of enabling those just on the threshold of owner-occupation to actually move into this tenure.

9 The Evolution of a Competitive Mortgage Market

The nature of the mortgage market in Britain has changed substantially over the past few years. Until the end of the 1970s, building societies were regarded as virtually monopoly suppliers of mortgage finance. Moreover, the mortgage market was almost continually short of funds, and it was accepted that one had to wait in a queue for a mortgage and to accept whatever loan terms were dictated by the building society. The changes in the mortgage market over the past few years are a part of a much wider change in the retail, wholesale, and, indeed, international financial markets. Within a few years the situation has been reached in which mortgages are freely available, on demand, from a variety of institutions to those able and willing to pay the price.

The Traditional Position

Building societies and the mortgage market have been almost synonymous. Going back to the 1950s and 1960s the mortgage market was quite small, partly because the level of owner-occupation was much lower than it is today. Building societies were the main providers of mortgage funds, the other significant lenders being the insurance companies and local authorities. The banks provided a limited amount of finance, not through special mortgage loans as such, but rather as a part of their normal lending procedures. A particularly significant role was played by the banks in respect of bridging finance, where people temporarily needed to finance the ownership of two houses, and banks also made loans to their staff, which in aggregate were a substantial amount. The savings banks did not lend at all, let alone for house purchase. Insurance companies gradually withdrew from the market, as mortgages were no longer appropriate for the portfolio which they wished to hold. In particular, mortgage rates were below other rates available. Building societies, therefore, found themselves, somewhat accidentally, in the position of monopoly suppliers.

It is necessary to examine, in some detail, why this situation occurred, because in most other countries there is a variety of mortgage lenders, including specialist building society type institutions, mortgage banks, commercial banks, savings banks, and co-operative banks. Building societies' gradual dominance of the market did not reflect their own characteristics, but rather reflected factors relating to the other potential lenders, the commercial banks and the savings banks.

It is proper to examine the savings banks first, as in most countries they are very large lenders and in some countries they are the largest lenders. In Britain, the savings banks, in the form of the trustee savings banks and the Post Office Savings Bank, which was renamed the National Savings Bank in 1969, have been under government control. In itself, this should not prevent savings banks from playing a full role in the financial markets. State-controlled savings banks in West Germany, France and many other countries are among the most active of financial institutions. However, in Britain, the government regarded the savings banks as merely a source of cheap funds. Interest rates were kept very low, and the banks handed over to the government all the savings which they collected. They had no lending function at all. The savings banks had difficulty in retaining their balances, and their market share fell very sharply. It is estimated that in 1950 they accounted for some 45 per cent of the liquid assets of the personal sector, but by 1980 the total amount held in savings banks and National Savings had fallen to under 20 per cent. One of the main competitors of building societies was, therefore, removed from the market by government action, or, rather, was not allowed to take its full place in the market because of government inaction.

The reason why the commercial banks have not been significant mortgage lenders also is related to government regulation. By the end of the 1950s, the importance of the money supply, as an economic variable, was being recognized. It became generally accepted that an increase in the supply of money above the increase in output of the economy was likely to lead to inflation, and government policy concentrated on controlling the money supply. This was taken to equate with bank deposits or bank lending, one being seen as the natural counterpart of the other. In 1960 this may have been a correct assumption because the banks dominated the financial markets. The government attempted to restrict bank activity, first by imposing ceilings on lending, and, more recently, in the 1970s, through what was known as the supplementary special deposit scheme, or the corset, which controlled the growth of the interest-bearing liabilities of the banks. Generally, government policy was aimed at limiting the growth of the balance sheets at the banks. This naturally made the banks unwilling to take on new business, because to the extent that they did so, they were penalized. In the case of the wholesale markets, which were becoming increasingly sophisticated, the controls were circumvented. For example, instead of banks taking in deposits from one company and lending them to another, the transaction thereby being recorded on the balance sheet of the bank, the banks simply guaranteed the issue of a bill by the institution with a shortage of funds, and arranged for it to be purchased by the institution with a surplus of funds, taking a commission for so doing. However, the retail markets do not lend themselves to such sophistication. The banks gradually reduced their retail activities. Their savings rates were uncompetitive compared with those of building societies and they lent only a small amount to individuals. This philosophy was reflected in the decision taken in the late 1960s to close bank branches on Saturday mornings.

The other institutions in the mortgage market were the local authorities. Many authorities believed that as part of their general housing service they should offer mortgage finance covering the whole range of properties available, while others took the view that building societies did not fully cater for the needs of borrowers acquiring cheap, inner-city, pre-1919 properties and that they should lend on these properties in particular. In the lax monetary conditions of the early 1970s local authority lending grew so that in 1974 they undertook more than a quarter of all net lending. Public expenditure constraints introduced in 1975 brought the growth of local authority lending to an abrupt halt. By 1976 only 3 per cent of new lending came from the authorities, and the establishment of the local authority support scheme meant that those house purchasers who previously would have borrowed from an authority were referred to a building society. Societies in general made a special allocation of funds to help people who the local authority felt were in priority categories and who might not obtain a loan under normal lending criteria.

By the late 1970s building societies were writing over 95 per cent of new mortgage business, and they were in the position of having to face little or no competition from their two principal potential competitors, the savings banks and the commercial banks, or from public sector agencies. This was at a time when the mortgage market was growing rapidly in response to the growth of owner-occupation and the increasing acceptance that house purchase was the most sensible investment any individual could make. In these circumstances building societies were able to make very comfortable profits. Moreover, the situation lent itself to restrictions on competition, with the objective of ensuring what, to the suppliers of mortgages – the building societies – were orderly market conditions but which to others would be seen as a cartel. The Building Societies Association had, in fact, been recommending to its members rates of interest which they should pay and charge since the late 1930s. The force of these recommendations became stronger, such that in the 1950s, 1960s and 1970s interest rates were, in effect, determined centrally by The Building Societies Association, with all the large societies effectively following those rates.

The rates recommended by The Building Societies Association were generally less than at a market clearing level. Moreover, they were very sticky, being slow to follow other interest rates, either up or down. Partly, the mortgage rate was kept below a market clearing level because it proved easier for societies to operate in a profitable manner with the existence of mortgage queues, although whether this was widely recognized in the industry at the time is debatable. The mortgage rate was also a subject of intense public and political interest, something which is inevitable with a variable rate mortgage system where the rate is determined not primarily by reference to any index of interest rates or to market rates but rather by the decisions of the lenders. There was considerable public pressure on building societies to keep mortgage rates down, and little consideration was given to the rate of interest which should properly be paid to investors.

The government acquiesced in these arrangements, and indeed considerable pressure was exerted on building societies on a number of occasions to hold interest rates at an artificially low level. Such pressure was particularly pronounced at election times. For example, in 1973, the Conservative government made building societies a modest grant in order to hold the mortgage rate below the politically sensitive level of 10 per cent. This was successful for a short time, but a further rise in market interest rates necessitated an increase in the mortgage rate to 11 per cent shortly thereafter. In 1974, immediately after the February election, which Labour won with a majority which was so small that a further election was clearly only a short time away, the new government lent building societies £500 million at a low rate of interest, in exchange for the mortgage rate not being increased.

The public perception at this time was that a low mortgage rate helped house buyers and the housing market. There seemed to be no acceptance that the main beneficiaries of a low mortgage rate were existing house owners, rather than new house purchasers. The effect of holding down the mortgage rate on the supply of funds, and therefore on the ability of people to purchase houses at all, was simply not recognized by many.

By the end of the 1970s, the mortgage market had become huge but remained unsophisticated in comparison with other markets. Prices were not responsive to supply and demand; the lenders, the building societies, were not responsive to what the consumer wanted, and the process of borrowing could be a long drawn-out affair. Potential house buyers were advised that if they wished to obtain a loan then they should first have a savings account with the building society. Inevitably, as in any situation where there is a shortage, quasi-blackmarket activities developed, and methods of queue jumping were devised. Financial intermediaries, such as estate agents, accountants and solicitors, were able to introduce investment funds to building societies in exchange for a quota of mortgage loans. Some argued that the local authority support scheme was a queue-jumping exercise. Those who knew the system were able to get the mortgage that they wanted. Others sometimes had to wait, or alternatively were forced to go to a fringe lender and pay a higher rate of interest. However, this was not in any way thought to be an undesirable situation. The public preoccupation was in keeping the mortgage rate down and governments, perhaps wisely, recognized that some 5 million existing mortgage holders had substantially more votes than perhaps 50,000 frustrated house buyers, many of whom believed that government attempts to keep the mortgage rate down were to their benefit.

Reasons for the Breakdown of the Traditional Position

The transition from the cartelized mortgage market which existed in the late-1970s to the competitive market which had emerged by the mid-1980s resulted from a combination of factors which affected the financial markets generally, rather than being specific to building societies.

Perhaps underlying all of these factors has been technology. Developments in the processing of information and in the communication of data have served to revolutionize financial services industries throughout the world. The small investor in a provincial town can now have access to the same information as a leading stockbroker in New York or London. Financial services which previously required complex computer systems, which could be afforded only by large banks, can now be made available through micro-computers in small institutions. Money can now be shifted instantaneously by electronic means, and this applies to individuals able to use automated teller machines (ATMs) as well as to large corporate investors.

These technological developments have helped break down the lines of demarcation between the various financial institutions. For example, previously it was possible to offer a retail banking service only through a large network of branches, and the largest British clearing banks have between 2,000 and 3,000 branches each. Technology, in the form of ATMs, makes branches less necessary, and it is now possible to provide a complete retail banking service with no branches at all, access to cash being obtained through automated teller machines, and other transactions being carried out by cheque or by credit card. This has opened up the retail banking industry, not just to building societies, but also to merchant banks, unit trust companies and American banks, which have some expertise in this area and now see the advantage of offering a low-cost service, while their main competitors, the banks, are still encumbered by cost structures appropriate to market conditions which no longer exist.

The second major factor has been deregulation and the commitment on the part of the Conservative government elected in 1979 to the operation of market forces. This government, as one of its first acts in 1979, abolished foreign exchange controls. The maintenance of balance sheet constraints on the banks then became pointless, because they could be circumvented through international operations. The abolition of the corset followed in 1980 and the banks were, for the first time, completely free of artificial balance sheet constraints.

These forces coincided with a development of a more competitive attitude on the part of some building societies. Cartels generally break down as a result of both internal and external pressure. By 1980, there was external pressure on the building societies because of the threat of bank competition in the mortgage market, and also because the government was making increasing use of National Savings to fund its borrowing requirement and this posed a competitive threat to societies in the savings market. Some societies saw their market shares being threatened and they were reluctant to continue at the pace of the slowest societies. Some societies also saw their opportunity to use the cartel to increase their market share at the expense of others. This is naturally easiest for smaller societies, as the impact which they can have on the larger ones is scarcely noticeable, whereas if a large society steps out of line, then all societies are immediately affected. A number of societies had developed the practice of operating on rates of interest above the recommended rates. They were able to offer a slightly higher than normal rate of deposits, which they then advertised, often without great expense. This additional cost could easily be borne by charging a higher than normal mortgage rate, and the market would accept this, because there was a permanent shortage of mortgage funds. Larger societies could not use this tactic, but, instead, they tended to observe the recommended rates only on traditional products, and simultaneously they introduced new products which they regarded as not being within the collective agreements.

In 1974, term shares had been introduced paying a rate of interest above the recommended ordinary share rate in exchange for the investor agreeing to leave his funds untouched for a period of between two and five years. In 1977 these accounts were brought within the recommended rates system, but they rapidly gained in importance and by the end of the 1970s withdrawal terms were being liberalized, such that effectively investors could obtain a higher than normal rate of interest on what were almost ordinary share accounts. Various short notice accounts outside the recommended rates system were also introduced by many societies from 1980, and ordinary shares declined as a proportion of total balances from 80 per cent in 1978 to 60 per cent in 1980 and down to under 20 per cent by the end of 1985. On the mortgage side, differential mortgage rates were introduced outside the BSA arrangements, with societies charging a higher than normal rate of interest for larger loans. This is of course exactly the opposite of what one expects, in that normally larger sums qualify for quantity discounts. Again, societies were able to get away with this and indeed it made sense for them to do so, because the market would accept higher mortgage rates for larger loans.

By the early 1980s the cartel was visibly dissolving. Funds were increasingly being raised at rates other than the recommended share rate, and loans were increasingly being made other than at the recommended mortgage rate. Societies had recognized that the future did not lie in attempting to seek an accommodation with their fellow competitors, but rather in seeking to compete against them, using all of the marketing opportunities that were available.

The Development of Competition in the 1980s

Competition in the mortgage market emerged both within the building society industry and also between building societies and banks. It is difficult to disentangle the two effects.

1980 was probably the benchmark year. It was in that year that the corset was finally abolished and the banks realized that they were free to compete on equal terms with building societies. Also in that year, the increase in short notice deposit accounts offered by building societies cast increasing doubt on the validity of the recommended rate arrangements, and The Building Societies Association established a committee to review the capital structure of building societies. In September 1981, the Council of the Association adopted that committee's recommendations, which were to limit the recommended share rate simply to the ordinary share rate, and to eliminate the requirement on societies to give twenty-eight days' notice of changes in deposit rates except for funds on less than twenty-eight days' notice.

The first thrust by the commercial banks into the mortgage market came in 1981. They had taken just 8 per cent of the market in 1980, a fairly typical figure for the 1970s. Their lending more than quadrupled in 1981 and they took 26 per cent of the market, their share rising even further to 40 per cent early in 1982. The banks concentrated on the most profitable part of the market, that is the market for large loans, where building societies charged higher interest rates. They also emphasized in their advertising that, unlike building societies, they could make decisions quickly. By this time the banks had clearly seen the mortgage market as a profitable market in its own right, with an exceptionally low bad debt record. Probably more importantly, the banks saw mortgage business as their way back into the personal market. They hoped that mortgage lending would lead to an increased flow of deposits and would enable them to capture related business such as insurance and unsecured lending.

The success of the banks was far greater than they had expected and by 1982 mortgage loans were taking an uncomfortably high proportion of net new lending, and mortgage balances were approaching the level that the banks felt reasonable in relation to their balance sheets generally. This led to a sharp reduction in bank mortgage lending over the next few years, the level of advances falling 60 per cent between 1982 and 1984 and the banks' market share falling from 36 per cent to 11 per cent over the same period. There was much criticism of the banks for moving in and out of the mortgage market as it suited them, and generally this initial foray into the market showed that the banks had not really done their research, and had not realized that they were entering a market which was quite unlike their other lending markets in that there was a virtually infinite demand, because the price was still below what was a market clearing level.

The initial move by the banks into the market had led many building societies to abandon the practice of differential mortgage rates. As the banks retreated somewhat from the market, so the practice of differential rates re-emerged and many were of the belief that the banks would no longer be significant mortgage lenders.

In the autumn of 1983, as bank lending was declining, so competition amongst building societies to obtain funds to meet the mortgage demand increased. The recommended rate system operated by The Building Societies Association came under further pressure when the second largest society, the Abbey National, announced that it no longer intended to be bound by the recommendations. The Association decided that in future its recommendations on interest rates would simply be replaced by advice; this may seem to be a semantic difference, but in reality was a very important one given the way that the BSA operated.

In July 1984, the government Green Paper, *Building Societies: A New Framework*, marked the first official statement by the government that it welcomed competition between building societies and in the mortgage market. The government announced that it intended to remove from building societies the exemption from Restrictive Trades Practices legislation which the interest rate agreements had enjoyed. This did indeed mark a very significant change in policy from that of the 1970s. The government had by this time recognized that holding the mortgage rate down was not necessarily desirable in itself. The government also saw that the artificial fixing of interest rates had an undesirable effect on the competitiveness and innovativeness of the financial system. As the banks had been freed from the constraints under which they operated, so they had become more responsive to the needs of consumers and the government considered that building societies would react similarly. This announcement by the government, in fact, led to a further bout of competition between building societies, such that by the end of the year The Building Societies Association had ceased even to advise interest rates. However, it did give advice on the magnitude and timing of changes in rates although with no specific figures being mentioned.

Towards the end of 1984, and more particularly in 1985, bank lending on mortgage increased again. It was not only the British clearing banks that were active in the market, but also American banks and foreign banks generally. This return to the mortgage market by the banks was part of the process of adapting to a new market where originally there had been overkill, followed by too severe a retreat. Some commentators were predicting that the banks would take between 20 per cent and 25 per cent of the market in the long term, a pattern which is evident in many other countries. By this time, mortgage rates had become much more responsive to market rates, as building societies generally had become more responsive to market conditions. The mortgage was seen as being a good investment, with a virtually nil chance of default and a rate of interest that appeared to be settling down at a significant margin over money market rates. Many international banks had huge sterling assets and were looking for profitable investment opportunities, and were increasingly attracted towards the mortgage market. The second surge of bank activity, therefore, reflected these factors as well as the more general wish of the High Street banks to restore their position in the personal market.

By mid-1985, a fully competitive mortgage market had emerged. Lenders were openly advertising for business and there was limited competition on loan terms. Some building societies began to change the rates they offered to new borrowers without reference to The Building Societies Association. For a time in mid-1985 the banks were more competitive than building societies, and this resulted in some redemptions of building society mortgage loans, with bank loans being taken out to replace them. Societies responded by abolishing differential mortgage rates again, this time probably permanently.

Bank lending declined again late in 1985 to levels that seemed to be well below the targets the banks had established earlier in the year. During the first few months of 1986 the banks made a greater effort to capture market share than at any time since their initial entry in 1981. Early in the year the banks abolished the differential traditionally charged on endowment loans, at little cost to themselves as they apparently had a relatively small proportion of their loans written on this basis. For building societies the situation was more serious in that over 50 per cent of their mortgage balances were linked to endowment policies. Nevertheless they had little option but to follow the lead of the banks, and thus the last remaining rationing device left over from the days of mortgage queues was abolished.

In a flurry of bank announcements in the spring of 1986 Midland Bank perhaps went the furthest in attempting to obtain new business. Not only did it abolish the endowment differential, but also it announced that it would, for a three-month period, pay the legal and valuation fees incurred by borrowers who wished to transfer their existing loans from other institutions to Midland. There were some allegations that business was being 'poached' by the bank, but the move may signal the end of the last obstacle to a truly efficient mortgage market in which existing balances as well as new loans are allocated by borrowers to the cheapest providers of funds. In the past most borrowers have been 'locked in' to their original institution until they moved house, as the costs of transferring a mortgage are such as to wipe out the gains of cheaper borrowing for some years. Also, there was no guarantee that the new institution would remain the cheapest source of funds in the period after the transfer had been completed. The removal of transactions costs in this area would ensure that lenders could not charge existing or new borrowers anything other than the market rate.

As well as marking a further increase in competition the first half of 1986 was also a period of rapidly declining interest rates. The competitive nature of the market meant that many societies wished to react to the situation without conferring with their competitors in The Building Societies Association. In mid-March the two largest societies reduced their mortgage rates, for both new and existing borrowers, before the Association had been able to make an announcement on the subject. At its April meeting the Association's Council decided that it should no longer seek to influence building society rates, and that individual boards of directors must bear the responsibility for deciding their own society's rates in the light of market conditions. The last vestiges of a cartelized market were therefore formally removed, although The Building Societies Association's Council did decide that it should continue to discuss general trends in the markets in which societies operate.

Table 9.1 shows how the market shares of banks and building societies in the mortgage market developed from 1978.

Table 9.1 *Net Loans for House Purchase 1978–85*

Year	*Percentage of total*	
	Building societies	*Monetary sector*
1978	94.1	5.1
1979	81.6	9.1
1980	78.1	6.8
1981	66.7	23.9
1982	57.6	35.9
1983	75.8	25.3
1984	86.4	13.7
1985	79.1	22.8

Source: CSO, 1986a.

Note: In 1983 and 1985 there were net repayments of loans to local authorities and the banks and building societies therefore accounted for more than 100 per cent of net lending.

The Consequences of a Competitive Mortgage Market

The major effects of the competitive mortgage market have already become apparent. Potential borrowers no longer have to save with an institution before hoping to borrow from it, mortgage queues have disappeared, and mortgages are sold like any other product to those willing and able to pay the price.

The major consequences of the changes can be grouped under three headings:

(1) An increase in the rate of innovation.
(2) A reduction in profit margins.
(3) An increase in risk.

In the 1960s and 1970s building societies had little incentive to introduce new mortgage products. The demand for their existing products, the repayment and endowment mortgage, was greater than societies could meet and there was no need for them to meet competition with product innovation. The situation had changed by the middle 1980s and the potential borrower was beginning to be offered a choice between different products. Early in 1986, for example, a few, relatively small lenders introduced mortgage loans with rates of interest linked to wholesale money market rates. The borrower was therefore certain that his repayments would fluctuate with the general level of rates in the economy, thus removing totally the discretion of the lender. At the other extreme, in April 1986 Lloyds Bank introduced a mortgage on which the interest rate was fixed for a three-year term. At the time it was introduced, mortgage rates were falling, and the rate was fixed at just over 1 per cent below the market rate for variable rate mortgages. Borrowers were therefore offered the chance of gambling on the future course of interest rates.

There were also innovations in the marketing of mortgages. In the 1960s and 1970s marketing was unnecessary, and in 1982 Lloyds Bank was able to claim that it was the first institution to advertise on television for mortgage business, an extraordinary state of affairs for a consumer product already used by six million people. By 1986 many building societies were undertaking extensive advertising campaigns and a number of sales aids had been introduced. Some lenders offered mortgage certificates guaranteeing to potential borrowers that funds would be available to them when they found the house they wanted (although it may be noted in passing that such certificates would have been much more useful in the rationed mortgage market of the 1970s, than in a period when funds were readily available). In contrast to the position before 1982 most building societies, by 1986, were allowing borrowers to see the valuation report (which they had paid for). Also, many lenders offered lower rates to first-time buyers for the first year of their mortgage. The Abbey National Building Society went further in establishing a 'property service' which gave members certain discounts on professional fees and furnishing costs.

The second consequence of the more liberalized market is the reduction in profit margins. In the absence of competition and using the cartel arrangements, building societies were able to choose their own profit margins during the 1960s and 1970s (with occasional outside interest from bodies such as the Prices and Incomes Board which conducted an investigation into building society reserves and profitability in 1966). Societies were able to expand their branch networks without any fear that they would become unprofitable, because over-expansion could be funded through a wider margin if necessary, although as with some of the other factors examined earlier in this chapter there is some doubt as to whether this was generally recognized at the time. The increase in competition has been accompanied by a marked slow down in branch expansion and a reduction in societies' management expense ratios, although this latter development is also related to the decline in inflation in recent years. The essential point is that whereas in the past societies were able to decide what level of costs they should bear and what profits they required, in the future the market will dictate to them their gross margins and they will need to contain their costs within that margin to produce an acceptable profit.

Finally, a more competitive market means that lenders are forced to take greater, although still by no means large, risks. In the 1970s building societies were able to pick and choose their borrowers, rejecting those who appeared to offer anything other than the very highest level of security. In an effort to obtain market share, most lenders now offer loans equal to 100 per cent of the purchase price, which obviously provides a lesser margin of security than a lower percentage advance. The restrictions on income multipliers have also tended to be competed away, so that marginal borrowers are now able to commit a high proportion of their earnings to repayments. It is also argued by some that, in an environment in which branch managers have targets rather than quotas for lending, fraudulent mortgage applications are less likely to be thoroughly investigated. The arrears and repossession statistics (see Chapter 7) illustrate the problems that can arise, and while the bulk of the increase in both measures can be attributed to rising unemployment, a more relaxed lending policy must also be associated with the rise in the figures.

The overall conclusion must be that the change in market conditions has been beneficial both for the institutions concerned and the borrowers they serve. The new environment puts a premium on efficiency and those institutions with higher administrative costs or inefficient mortgage services are under a pressure to change that did not exist before. Borrowers no longer face queues, restrictions, lack of product choice, or paternalistic branch managers. Rather, they are confronted by a range of institutions offering a large number of different types of mortgage, with branch managers eager to serve them in order to obtain business. The mortgage market has become similar to that for any other consumer product.

10 The Emergence of Securitization and Secondary Market Activity

A major trend in financial markets throughout the world has been the securitization of loans. This means that a tradeable security is created with the payments of principal and interest on the original loans used to service the security. Securitization has advantages for both borrowers and lenders. Lenders have a more liquid instrument while borrowers are able to obtain finer margins over market rates of interest. Generally, securitization has not extended to mortgage markets for a number of reasons, not least the peculiar nature of mortgage loans. However, there is a thriving secondary mortgage market in the United States, and recently signs have emerged of conditions favouring the establishment of at least quasi-secondary market activity in Britain.

The Concept of Securitization and Secondary Markets

The standard mortgage loan in Britain is an instrument which is generally understood. That is, a lender makes a loan to enable the borrower to purchase the house. The lender holds the loan in his own portfolio and collects monthly repayments of interest and, where appropriate, principal. In the event of default the lender seeks to take possession of the property. A typical mortgage loan in Britain carries a rate of interest which is variable at the discretion of the lender, although the extent to which a lender can stand against market forces is increasingly limited.

Securitization and secondary market activity are slightly different in nature but very similar in effect. Taking secondary market activity first, this simply means that a lender, having made a loan in the traditional way, sells the loan to another institution wishing to hold mortgage loans. The original lender might prefer to continue servicing the loan, or the servicing could be transferred to the new lender. With this concept a mortgage loan is rather similar in some respects to a gilt-edged security, in that the holder of the instrument is able to sell it to another party. However, the big difference is that in the case of gilts there is just one borrower and many thousands of lenders. In the case of mortgage loans, by contrast, there are many thousands of borrowers and a much fewer number of lenders.

Securitization differs from secondary market activity in that the loan itself is not sold but rather a security is created backed by the principal and interest payments on the loan. Through this means the beneficial ownership of the loan is effectively transferred. The purchaser of the loan assumes the risk in the event of loan default, and the lender removes the risk from its balance sheet.

Once securitization has taken place, then the securities themselves can be traded in a secondary market. The main difference between securitization and a secondary market without securitization is simply one of sophistication. Where whole loans are sold then this is generally a one-off transaction, perhaps for a special reason, but securitization implies a permanent market in the securities. It is important to understand this distinction because often there is confusion between securitization and secondary market activity, and indeed also for that matter between secondary market activity and wholesale borrowing. For example, British building societies have recently been borrowing substantial sums on the Eurobond market on an unsecured basis. American savings associations and quasi-governmental agencies have been borrowing funds on the Eurobond market backed by mortgages. The instruments are similar but the underlying security is quite different, mortgages in the case of the American savings and loan associations, but the whole of the assets in the case of British building societies.

To many in Britain, the concept of securitization or of selling loans is an alien one. There is a feeling that people take out a mortgage loan with a particular institution and would be loath to see that institution sell the loan to another institution. However, in practice what people have is a loan and it is that which is the product, rather than the loan from a specific bank or building society. It should make no difference to the borrower who holds the loan. What actually matters is the terms on which the loan is made. One has to qualify the statement slightly because of the variable rate nature of British mortgage loans. With a rate of interest which can be varied at any time by the lender, then a borrower is to some extent relying on the goodwill of his lender. This argument remains a fairly powerful one emotionally, although in an increasingly competitive market place it probably now has much less force. If any lender tries to maintain loan rates even to existing borrowers above the prevailing market rate, then that institution would very rapidly lose business to others.

The Secondary Market in the USA

In only one country in the world, the USA, is there a significant secondary market in residential mortgage loans. About one half of all mortgage loans are traded, and mortgage-backed securities are now a major part of the financial markets. Some see the situation in America as the forerunner of that in other industrialized countries, and many of the institutions which are major secondary market operators in America are already established in

London and other financial centres and no doubt would like to be able to use tried and tested American techniques in other markets. However, in analysing the American secondary market it is necessary to understand the peculiar circumstances which have bought about that market.

America is a federal country and the individual states have considerable autonomy, including with respect to the regulation of financial institutions. It is still generally the position that financial institutions are unable to branch outside their state of origin, and in some states, for example Illinois, there are restrictions on branching within states. One of the main purposes of financial institutions is to shift funds from capital surplus areas to capital deficit areas. In Britain and in most other countries, funds are shifted around the country within financial institutions because they operate on a nation-wide basis. However, this has not been true in the USA. As the West and, more recently, the South expanded rapidly so they found they were unable to satisfy their capital requirements from within their regions. Rather, finance had to be sought from the more well-established East Coast. Secondary market activity developed for this reason. Loans were originated in the West and the South and sold to institutions in the East. Often this was done through a correspondent banking system, and this was even used to sell loans to institutions in Britain and other countries.

Secondly, the USA has had heavily regulated financial markets. Many states have imposed usury ceilings which have limited the ability of lenders to obtain a satisfactory rate of return on mortgage loans. Such financial institutions, therefore, have often sought to purchase mortgage loans from other states which have yielded a more satisfactory rate of return.

Finally, and more generally, with a few modest exceptions, until recently American mortgage lenders were unable to charge variable rates of interest. However, they had to raise their money on a variable rate basis. This laid them open to the classic banking trap of borrowing short and lending long. One way that the institutions could reduce this risk was to originate loans but then to sell them to those better equipped to hold long-term loans.

These various forces led to the emergence of a huge secondary market assisted by the operation of a number of quasi-governmental agencies, which have helped to establish uniform lending criteria, and which have also provided liquidity to the mortgage market and helped stimulate the development of effective markets in both mortgages and mortgage-backed securities.

Currently, nearly one-third of residential mortgage loans in the United States are originated by institutions known as mortgage banks or mortgage companies. These institutions simply have the function of originating loans which they then pool together and either sell whole, or sell as securities backed by those loans. The mortgage banks continue to service the loans, and they derive their income from servicing and origination fees, rather than from the interest margin. Many savings associations act as mortgage bankers themselves, especially where they make fixed rate loans which they prefer not to hold on their balance sheet. The savings institutions are now able to make variable rate loans and naturally they are more inclined to hold these loans on their balance sheets as they can be matched by variable rate deposits.

Mortgage-backed securities and whole mortgage loans are purchased by institutional investors such as insurance companies and pension funds. They are also purchased by the mortgage lenders themselves who may prefer to hold securities on their balance sheets rather than actual loans. To the institutional investor, mortgage loans are attractive because they carry a rate of interest higher than government securities or commercial paper. There is a risk of default, but so sophisticated is the market and such are the lending standards that have to be met, that this is fairly modest and can be predicted fairly accurately.

To the institutional investor, the one problem is early repayment. Most instruments which are traded in the wholesale financial markets have a fixed maturity and cannot be redeemed prematurely. However, it is impossible to stop a house purchaser redeeming a mortgage loan. What has happened in America is that institutions which help to make the secondary market work calculate the likely repayment pattern, so the institutional investor at least knows the phasing of loan repayments. More recently there has been the development of collaterized mortgage obligations (CMOs). The borrowers' payments are paid into a single pool. Interest payments are passed on to investors. However, principal repayments are passed on to investors class by class, with one class being paid off entirely before any principal is repaid to the next greater maturity class. Investors can therefore choose with a fair degree of accuracy the maturity of the instruments which they are purchasing.

It is fair to say that the secondary market in America exists primarily because of imperfections in the primary market. There is no doubt that even without the intervention of government agencies there would be quite significant trading in whole loans. What the various government agencies have done is to promote securitization. There are three major agencies:

(1) The Government National Mortgage Association (GNMA, 'Ginnie Mae') which is part of the Department of Housing and Urban Development. This guarantees loans made by approved lenders, generally mortgage banks. The lenders are fully responsible for servicing the loans and also for the marketing and administration of the securities backed by the loans. GNMA earns its income through a simple guarantee fee. To the institutional investor, GNMA securities are in effect as good as government securities because they are fully backed by the government.
(2) The Federal National Mortgage Association (FNMA, 'Fannie Mae')

purchases mortgage loans, which it holds on its own portfolio, and it raises its funds through issues of debentures and short-term discount notes. More recently it has begun to sell securities backed by mortgages.

(3) The Federal Home Loan Mortgage Corporation (FHLMC, 'Freddie Mac' or the Mortgage Corporation) purchases loans and then resells the loans by means of mortgage participation certificates. Unlike FNMA it does not hold loans on its balance sheet.

'Fannie Mae' and 'Freddy Mac' have helped to establish uniform lending criteria which lenders must meet if loans are to be purchased by the two institutions. Government insurance also plays an important part. The Federal Housing Administration insures loans and the Veterans Administration guarantees them, and most of the early secondary market activity was in respect of these loans. More recently, privately insured mortgage loans have also been securitized, as have uninsured loans, although these have to be for a fairly low percentage of the value of the property.

The Rationale for Securitization in Britain

In examining the rationale for securitization of mortgage loans in Britain it is necessary to look at what may be described as latent factors which have been present in the housing finance market for some time, and then at developments which have emerged over the past few years and which seem likely to precipitate secondary market activity. It is helpful in beginning the analysis to split the housing finance function into three fairly distinct components:

(1) Originating the loan. This involves a credit assessment of the borrower and a valuation of the property, together with all the necessary paperwork.

(2) The servicing of the loan. This involves the collection of the regular monthly repayments of principal and interest and passing them on to whomever is entitled to them. This function would also deal with any problems that arise during the life of the loan, for example, default and interest rate changes.

(3) Holding the loan. This involves raising and holding the funds used to finance the loan.

The three functions are very different and require different characteristics. Originating loans is best done by those institutions which have close contact with house buyers, for example estate agents. Servicing loans is fairly mechanical and can be done by any institution with a basic computer system and operations in the financial markets. Holding mortgage loans is obviously most profitable for institutions which can raise funds at the cheapest price.

Traditionally, in Britain all three functions have been carried out by building societies and they have become expert in the three functions together. However, this does not make them the most expert in each of the individual functions and what seems to be emerging is specialization within the various functions. A number of reasons explain this.

The first, and probably the most important, is the establishment of a market clearing rate for mortgages, as noted in the previous chapter. No longer are mortgage rates held at an artificially low level. When this was the case, there was no great wish on the part of general financial institutions and institutional investors to hold mortgage loans, simply because they were a poor investment. Over the past few years the mortgage rate has only dipped below money market rates for short periods of time and generally averaged over one percentage point above. The effect of this is that the mortgage loan is now attractive to institutional investors. It is likely to yield more than a government security or a commercial loan. This is especially true as the default record is excellent, and effectively residential mortgage loans can be regarded as a risk-free investment.

With the emergence of this situation, the other elements of securitization and quasi-secondary market activity fall into place. In the past, building societies were in a powerful position in the housing finance market, because they supplied the scarce commodity, mortgage loans. Other agents in the housing market, such as estate agents and housebuilders, eagerly sought mortgage quotas from building societies and societies were able to pick and choose the people with whom they did business. This is no longer the case. Rather, it is now the case that building societies seek mortgage business. Estate agents have very quickly become important in the housing finance market rather than in the narrow market in which they previously operated. The house buyer is likely to approach an estate agent before anyone else and the estate agent can, effectively, channel his customers to particular mortgage lenders.

Estate agents have no wish to hold mortgage loans, and in any event they are not equipped to do so. However, they do see opportunities to originate mortgage loans because this allows them to earn fees in other directions; for example, insurance commission and commission on the sale of other financial products.

Put very simply, the rationale for secondary market activity in Britain is that the mortgage instrument is now an attractive instrument for institutional investors and, for this reason alone, an industry is developing to meet the demands of institutional investors through supplying and servicing loans to those investors. The estate agents are at the forefront of this new activity as are building societies themselves.

Towards a Secondary Market

However, the British market needs to change quite considerably before there can be a significant amount of securitization. British mortgages as presently constituted give little scope for securitization or for sales of whole loans. The originators of mortgage loans have been the same as the holders, and therefore they have not had to satisfy a third party about the quality of their lending. There is no accepted underwriting criteria, no standardization of mortgage documentation and no common terms for the insurance of the top slice of mortgage loans.

Most importantly, the traditional British mortgage loan carries a rate of interest which is variable at the discretion of the lender and prepayment can occur at any time without penalty. It must be doubted if such an instrument can effectively be securitized, even if legally this is possible. A lender trying to sell a variable rate loan would find itself subjected to considerable criticism from its borrowers and from the media for exposing the borrowers to the vagaries of an alien financial institution. The purchasing institution could not be certain of the quality of its investment and might doubt its ability to vary the rate of interest in a way which would suit it. Here it must be noted that it makes little sense for loans to be sold with the rate of interest remaining at the discretion of the seller of the loan with the purchaser being entitled to a different rate. This would mean that the risk stayed with the original lender who therefore would have no advantage in selling the loan. The rationale for selling on the part of the vendor is to get the loan off its balance sheet because it does not suit its purposes to have it on the balance sheet.

This rather suggests that if there is to be secondary market activity in Britain, it will be in respect of new, rather than existing, loans which are tailor-made to suit the secondary market. Such loans would have to meet certain standards in respect of loan-to-value ratio and loan-to-income ratio, and there would have to be insurance of the top slice of loans on a commonly agreed basis. More importantly, it is difficult to see how loans can be securitized or sold while they are at a rate of interest which is variable at the discretion of the lender. This does not mean fixed rate loans, necessarily, though as Lloyds Bank illustrated in early 1986 there is scope for loans with a rate of interest that is fixed for, say, three years at a time. Rather, there must be scope for loans which are variable, but in relation to money market rates of interest, rather than at the discretion of the lender. A loan could, for example, carry a fixed premium over, say, three month LIBOR (LIBOR stands for London Inter Bank Offered Rate, one of the main indicators of the level of short term interest rates in the London money markets). The borrower would know exactly how his rate of interest was determined and the purchaser of a loan, or a security backed by a loan, would know that he would be getting a return related to money market rates.

It is difficult to deal with the prepayment problem, because it is impossible to prevent borrowers repaying their loans prematurely. Some investors might be prepared to accept this situation, especially as prepayment patterns could be carefully calculated. There might also be the scope for collateralized mortgage obligations on the American pattern, which would reduce the prepayment uncertainty.

It remains to be seen to what extent there will be securitization of mortgage loans and secondary market activity in Britain. As far as the principal participants in the mortgage market, the building societies, are concerned, these developments will not bring any great advantages to them. They are already able to raise whatever money they need from the wholesale markets on an unsecured basis, partly because their mutual nature means that they offer exceptionally good security to institutional investors. However, societies might find themselves coming under pressure in respect of their capital ratios, bearing in mind that new legislation will give them considerably wider powers, and some may find it increasingly profitable to derive their income from fees rather than the interest margin.

It is almost certain that the driving force behind securitization will not be the British building societies, but rather institutions which see the opportunity for raising very cheap wholesale money, and lending it in the British mortgage market, but without the expense of having to operate with substantial branch networks, and servicing large numbers of small loans. Investment bankers are therefore likely to try to introduce a secondary market and their allies in this are the estate agents, who should be able to generate mortgage business and related fee income without needing to hold the loans themselves, and the insurance companies, some of which have large sales forces and are able to sell insurance products related to mortgage lending.

PART IV

Policy Issues

11 Housing Finance and the Real Economy

The extent to which the operation of the housing finance market affects the level of activity in the wider economy has been the subject of debate for some years. This has been caused partly by the very size of the housing finance market. In 1985, for example, building societies made net advances of £14 billion, about double the size of the public sector borrowing requirement. Total mortgage debt outstanding at the end of 1985 was equivalent to about two-thirds of the national debt, while the total assets of all building societies at the same date were three times those of the electricity supply industry, one of the most capital-intensive industries in the UK.

Figures like these have led some commentators to assume that the housing or housing finance markets are absorbing resources at such a rate that other sectors of the economy are adversely affected. This argument was particularly popular in the mid-1970s, and was coupled with an idea that building societies were absorbing too great a proportion of the nation's savings to the detriment of other institutions undertaking more important lending activities. By the mid-1980s the debate had swung full circle and there was concern about the level of leakage from the housing finance market, that is, the use of funds nominally for house purchase for other purposes.

Real and Financial Resources

For the individual it is quite proper to add together the contents of bank and building society accounts, the value of stocks and shares held and the estimated value of televisions, refrigerators and cars to calculate the amount of wealth owned. It is not appropriate, however, to add together every individual's and company's physical and financial resources to discover the total wealth of the country. This fallacy of aggregation occurs because money is not a resource, but rather represents a command over resources or a means of exchanging resources.

Basically, the resources of an economy are people, skills and physical equipment, together with space to use these resources. In the economist's jargon they are labour, entrepreneurship, capital and land. An increase in the supply of labour will enable more goods to be produced and the economy will be wealthier as a result. However, if the government merely doubles the number of £5 notes in existence no real goods have been created. Only if overseas residents are willing to accept £5 notes in exchange for their goods will the economy become any wealthier. If the government is in the habit of doubling the number of bank notes in existence foreigners will be less willing to accept them and their value in relation to other currencies and in relation to goods and services will be reduced.

Real resources can be used only in one place at a time. For example, if the entire population of a country is engaged in producing butter, it is not possible for the economy also to produce aeroplanes. Similarly, if all resources are employed, an increase in the production of housing will necessitate a reduction in the output of the other goods, except over the long term, when it can be expected that efficiency in the use of resources will increase, leading to a greater output from the economy for a given input.

Housebuilding and the Use of Resources

In the middle of the 1970s it was common to hear arguments that housing was especially privileged. One clearing bank chairman was alleged to have said that Britain would have 'the best housed unemployed in Europe' because resources were being used to build houses that would have been better employed in manufacturing.

The extent to which resources are being used in the production of housing can be measured in a number of ways. It is possible to add up the number of men employed in house construction, the number of bricks used over a given time period, the amount of land developed and so on but it is not very easy to compare the totals obtained with other types of resources used in the rest of the economy. The most sensible thing to do is to convert the physical resources used into monetary values, with these money values representing the actual physical resources used. It is then possible to compare those money values with the money values of other resources used in the economy and this is done in the following pages. It is important to understand, however, that for the economy as a whole, money itself is not invested in housing; the actual investment is bricks and mortar, which are represented, for the sake of convenience, by their monetary equivalents. It follows, therefore, that it is not possible to compare the level of mortgage lending with, say, the output of the economy. Mortgage lending is a monetary variable, with no 'real' counterpart, merely facilitating, for the most part, the exchange of houses. Mortgage finance can be used to purchase newly built houses but this accounts for no more than about 12 per cent of new lending.

In order to assess the importance of housing in the economy it is possible either to look at the stock of housing existing and compare it with other forms of physical wealth such as factories, machinery, offices and vehicles, or to look at the flow of new resources into housing and to compare that with other flows in the economy. Such comparisons can be made at a given time or observed over a period of years. Comparisons can also be made with the position in other countries in order to assess whether the British situation is unusual in any way.

Assessing the stock of wealth held in the country is no easy task. It is relatively easy to add together the capital value of all machines installed in factories, all buildings used to produce goods and all dwellings used for people to live in. It is more difficult to assess the value of, say, the labour force, or of the entrepreneurial skills used in the organization of machines and labour to produce goods that people wish to buy. In the short analysis that follows this problem is ignored, and Table 11.1 shows the value of the capital stock in the UK over the latest eleven-year period for which data is available.

Table 11.1 *Gross Capital Stock at 1980 Replacement Cost, 1974–84*

Year	*Dwellings*		*Plant and machinery*		*Other buildings*		*Vehicles*		*Total*
	£bn	*%*	*£bn*	*%*	*£bn*	*%*	*£bn*	*%*	*£bn*
1974	287.5	30.9	230.8	24.8	364.8	39.2	48.3	5.2	931.4
1975	295.9	30.8	238.5	24.8	376.2	39.2	48.9	5.1	959.6
1976	304.5	30.8	246.4	24.9	387.7	39.2	49.3	5.0	987.8
1977	312.6	30.8	254.1	25.0	398.0	39.2	50.5	5.0	1,015.3
1978	320.9	30.8	262.4	25.2	407.9	39.1	51.5	4.9	1,042.7
1979	329.2	30.7	271.7	25.4	417.5	39.0	52.6	4.9	1,070.9
1980	336.8	30.7	280.6	25.6	426.3	38.8	53.7	4.9	1,097.3
1981	343.1	30.7	288.0	25.8	434.2	38.8	52.6	4.7	1,117.8
1982	349.8	30.7	295.4	25.9	443.1	38.9	51.4	4.5	1,139.7
1983	357.6	30.8	302.9	26.1	451.7	38.9	50.2	4.1	1,162.3
1984	365.2	30.7	310.7	26.2	461.8	38.9	50.1	4.2	1,187.8

Source: CSO, 1985, Table 11.9.
Notes: Vehicles includes road vehicles, railway rolling stock, ships and aircraft.

Housing accounts for about 30 per cent of Britain's capital stock, a slightly higher proportion than that for plant and machinery, but rather lower than for other buildings and works (such as offices and factories). The proportions have changed very little over the years, with dwellings exhibiting the least change. This perhaps is not surprising. Although stock comparisons are useful in assessing the importance of housing in relation to other sectors of the economy, they, in effect, show how resources have been used in the past. They provide a static comparison, because it is not possible, for example, to re-use the resources used in building a house when some other product is desired. The flow analysis can be more instructive because it shows the choices an economy makes in a particular year between various competing uses for resources.

Figures for investment in dwellings are available back to 1948. Table 11.2 compares investment in dwellings with total investment in the economy, and with the total output of the economy, for successive five-year periods. Perhaps the first surprising feature of the table is that investment in housing peaked in the 1968–1972 period. Indeed, dwellings' investment has never recovered its 1968 level of £9.8 billion. Housing as a proportion of GDP was also at a peak in the 1968–72 period, and accounted for a relatively high proportion of total investment, although on this measure housing was at its most important in the middle 1950s.

Table 11.2 *Investment in Dwellings, Total Investment and Gross Domestic Product (1980 Prices), 1948–84*

Year	*Investment in dwellings (annual averages)*			
	£m	*Per cent of GDP*	*Per cent of total investment*	*Average growth of GDP, per cent per annum*
1948–52	3,299	3.5	24.0	2.6
1953–57	4,642	4.2	25.3	3.1
1958–62	5,064	4.1	21.1	2.5
1963–67	7,668	5.2	23.5	3.4
1968–72	9,396	5.6	23.5	2.4
1973–77	9,188	4.9	21.8	2.2
1978–82	8,354	4.2	20.3	0.6
1983–84	8,934	4.3	20.5	2.4

Source: CSO, 1986b, Tables 13 and 51.

There is some correlation between the proportion of GDP devoted to housing and the rate of growth of GDP; the 1963–7 period did have a high rate of economic growth and high investment in dwellings, and investment in dwellings declined in the late 1970s and early 1980s as GDP growth declined. There is little evidence to suggest, however, that the devotion of resources to housing has in any way inhibited the growth of the economy.

Additional conclusions can be drawn by comparing the situation in the United Kingdom with that in the other major industrial countries. Table 11.3 shows the relevant data. The following three points emerge:

(1) The housing cycle in the other major industrial countries has followed a broadly similar pattern to that in the United Kingdom, with the importance of housing peaking in the 1974–9 period. West Germany and Italy stand out as having a somewhat different pattern, with housing being most important in the early 1960s.

(2) There is a correlation between the proportion of GDP invested in dwellings and the rate of growth of GDP. Thus in the UK and USA,

where economic growth has been relatively low since 1960, the proportion of output devoted to housing has been low. Canada has the next smallest growth of GDP and also the next lowest importance of housing. The relationship does not quite hold with the other countries: Japan has the highest economic growth rate, but the second highest proportion of resources devoted to housing, while Germany has the highest investment in dwellings, but the third highest economic growth rate.

(3) In each of the four periods Britain devoted a lower proportion of resources to residential construction than any of the other major economies of the world.

Table 11.3 *Residential Construction as Percentage of GDP and Growth of GDP, Major Countries, 1960–83*

	Residential construction as per cent of GDP				*Growth of GDP per capita, per cent per annum*
	1960–67	*1968–73*	*1974–79*	*1980–83*	*1960–83*
United Kingdom	3.5	4.0	4.2	3.5	1.9
USA	4.5	4.5	4.4	3.6	1.9
West Germany	7.3	7.2	6.0	6.5	2.8
France	5.7	6.8	6.9	5.8	3.3
Italy	6.0	5.9	5.3	5.3	3.2
Canada	4.4	5.0	5.9	5.3	2.7
Japan	5.2	7.2	7.6	6.2	6.0
All	4.9	5.4	5.5	4.7	2.8

Source: OECD, 1985b, Tables 3.2 and 6.9.
Note: The figures for the United Kingdom are different from those shown in Table 11.2 because of the exclusion of investment in repairs and improvement to dwellings.

It does seem likely that rather than residential construction holding back the development of the economy, the causation runs the other way, with a rapid rate of economic growth enabling countries to devote extra resources to housing. Furthermore, this also appears to be the case in the UK where there is some association between periods of strong economic growth and increases in the importance of investment in housing.

Housing Finance and the Flow of Funds

The previous section has shown that it is unlikely that investment in housing has been responsible for the poor performance of the UK economy in recent years. The idea that this might have been the case has probably resulted from the huge flows of funds through the housing market. The concept of a flow of funds through a market is important, in that the funds committed for house purchase do not just 'disappear' into a bottomless pit, but rather, having been used to facilitate an exchange, or a number of exchanges, of dwellings, generally become re-available for investment in some other area of the economy once the end of a housing chain is reached.

This concept of the 'last-time seller' was introduced in the BSA report (1979) and was explained briefly in Chapter 2. To recapitulate, most people selling a house will exchange it for funds which, usually along with a loan, will be used to purchase another dwelling. The people selling this dwelling will also use the proceeds of their sale to purchase another dwelling. In some cases such chains can have up to twenty links. At one end there will probably be a first-time buyer, putting resources into the housing market, while at the other end there will be a last-time seller, taking funds out of the market. This could result from the death of an elderly owner-occupier, where the beneficiaries of the will receive funds which are not reapplied to the housing market, or it could result from an owner-occupier moving down market or to another tenure, perhaps on retirement. The point is that the private housing market is able to absorb only those resources used in purchasing dwellings from other sectors of the economy, building new dwellings, repairing existing dwellings, or buying and selling homes (i.e. transactions resources). All other money put into the market must ultimately and eventually leave the market. In some years the money taken out of the market by last-time sellers will be equal to that put in, as deposits, by first-time buyers, with the rise in the number of owner-occupied homes and repairs being financed by lenders. In other years it is possible for first time-buyers' deposits to decline and for the amount lent to borrowers to be greater than the resources absorbed by the market in the four ways noted above. In this case the phenomenon known as equity withdrawal occurs.

Before examining in more detail the concept of equity withdrawal it is interesting to examine the flow and stock of funds involved in housing finance both in absolute terms and in relation to other flows and stocks in the economy. In contrast to the comparisons in the first part of this chapter this gives an idea, not of the resources devoted to housing in relation to the resources used elsewhere, but of the size of the housing finance market, that is, the funds used to exchange resources, in relation to the factors supporting the growth of the market, such as personal wealth and personal incomes.

On most comparative measures the housing finance market has been growing in size in recent years. Table 11.4 compares loans for house purchase outstanding with three separate indicators of the financial position of the personal sector.

Each of the measures shows an increase in the relative importance of mortgage debt since at least 1980, and in some cases, since the early 1960s.

Table 11.4 *Loans for House Purchase*

Year	*% of financial liabilities*	*% of net wealth*	*% of value of dwellings*
1957	50.0	6.5	27.8
1962	46.5	6.3	23.6
1967	53.5	6.5	22.0
1972	57.4	7.1	19.3
1977	60.4	8.3	19.9
1980	58.0	7.8	16.2
1981	58.2	8.5	17.9
1982	60.4	9.3	20.1
1983	61.0	9.7	21.0
1984	62.2	10.2	22.2

Source: CSO, 1986c, Table S2; Committee to Review the Functioning of Financial Institutions, 1980, Appendices, Table 10.

Borrowing for house purchase accounted for over 62 per cent of all borrowing at the end of 1984, compared with only 58 per cent in 1980 and only 46 per cent in 1962. Similarly, home loans are now equivalent to 10 per cent of net wealth (i.e. physical and financial assets minus financial liabilities), compared to 8 per cent in 1980 and 6 per cent in 1962. The trends in both these variables reflect not only the growth in owner-occupation, but also the recent liberalization of the mortgage market. That mortgage borrowing has grown more rapidly than other borrowing in recent years is perhaps slightly surprising given the extent of deregulation in the other credit markets, and perhaps reflects the relative lack of competition for unsecured lending business, compared to the, at times, intense competition for mortgages.

The third column of the table exhibits a somewhat different trend. Loans for house purchase accounted for well over a quarter of the value of dwellings owned by persons in the late 1950s, but following a long period of mortgage rationing, combined with rapid house price inflation, the proportion had fallen to around one-sixth by 1980. Since that year house price inflation has been low by the standards of the 1970s, while mortgage lending has grown rapidly, and by 1984 mortgage debt was equivalent to around a quarter of the estimated value of the private housing stock.

It is perhaps surprising to those accustomed to hearing of the proliferation of 100 per cent mortgages that of the £486 billion of dwellings held by persons in 1984, only £108 billion (22.2 per cent) is encumbered by mortgage debt (although some bank lending not for house purchase is secured on housing), leaving a potential secured lending market of £378 billion. One would expect to see a growth of secured lending, not necessarily related to house purchase, during the later 1980s.

There is one other ratio worth examining in assessing the importance of mortgage finance in the flow of funds in the wider economy. As might be expected the mortgage debt-to-income ratio has risen rapidly in recent years. Table 11.5 illustrates the trends. There has clearly been a dramatic escalation of mortgage borrowing in relation to income in recent years, which has undoubtedly been associated with the deregulation of the market. Whether this deregulation has encouraged people to borrow or merely enabled them to realize previously held desires is not clear.

Table 11.5 *Mortgage Debt/Personal Disposal Income Ratio*

Year	*Mortgage debt/ income* %	*Year*	*Mortgage debt/ income* %
1957	22.7	1980	32.4
1962	25.6	1981	35.2
1967	29.7	1982	39.9
1972	35.3	1983	44.4
1977	33.9	1984	48.9

Source: As for Table 11.3; CSO, 1986b.

Equity Withdrawal

The concept of equity withdrawal is a relatively simple one. It is the increase in mortgage debt less the value of additions to the owner-occupied stock. Very approximate calculations for the latter for 1985 are as follows:

Numbers of private houses completed (149,000) multiplied by average price of new houses (£38,000) = value of new private houses	£5.7 billion
+ Value of council houses transferred to owner-occupation (sales of 120,000 multiplied by average price of £12,750)	£1.5 billion
+ Value of improvement less depreciation	£4.0 billion
Total	£11.2 billion

It must be stressed that the figures are merely rough approximations. This applies particularly to the value of improvements less depreciation, which is no more than an intelligent guess. Nevertheless, the method of calculation is correct although it would be helpful if it could be refined to produce more accurate figures.

Net mortgage loans in 1985 were £18.1 billion. If £11.2 billion represented the value of the net increase in the stock then the remainder (£7 billion or 39 per cent) by definition represented equity withdrawn. Of this, probably around £1.5 billion would have been used to finance transactions costs.

The amount of equity withdrawn from the housing market has increased sharply in recent years. Bank of England estimates suggest that it accounted for just 15 per cent of net mortgage advances in the 1966–70 period before rising to 49 per cent in 1982.

Equity withdrawal can occur in a number of ways:

(1) By people borrowing on mortgage for purposes other than house purchase or improvement.
(2) By a person moving house and not reinvesting all of the proceeds in a new dwelling. For example, someone selling a £30,000 house with a £10,000 mortgage may buy a £40,000 house with a £30,000 mortgage. In this case equity of £10,000 (before allowing for transaction costs) has been withdrawn from the housing market and is available for expenditure or investment elsewhere.
(3) On death. When owner-occupiers die, they normally leave their estate to their children, who are also likely to be owner-occupiers. The house of the deceased person will be sold and the proceeds paid to the beneficiaries of the estate. Such beneficiaries may invest the money received or they may spend it.

The concept of equity withdrawal has been generally misunderstood in one important respect and criticized in two others. The misunderstanding has arisen from many commentators' assertion that half of all lending for house purchase is really for other purposes, the proportion being derived from the Bank of England's 1982 estimate. The practice has been criticized because it is believed that this proportion of lending has been illegally attracting tax relief and also because there is a feeling in some quarters that building societies should lend only for actual house purchase, rather than for other purposes.

It has not, in fact, been the case that building societies and other lending institutions have been financing other expenditure with tax-relieved housing finance. This is appreciated most easily when considering the case of people dying as owner-occupiers. A building society will make a completely bona fide 100 per cent loan of, say, £30,000 to possibly a first-time buyer to enable him to buy the house. No equity will have been put into the house by the buyer yet £30,000 will be taken out by the beneficiaries of the estate and this sum will be available for other uses. It is clearly wrong to restrict the availability of tax relief or to restrict lending to first-time buyers in this situation, and yet the result of the building society making the loan is that £30,000 becomes available for either financing consumption or investment in financial assets (possibly in the building society providing the original loan) or paying off other types of borrowing. Equity withdrawal is an inevitable consequence of people dying as owner-occupiers.

In the case of a person not reinvesting all the proceeds of a sale the arguments become more finely balanced. In times of mortgage shortage building societies have in the past insisted that those moving invest all of the 'profit' made on the sale of the first house in the new dwelling. The society was, in effect, making the borrower's decision for him on the level of indebtedness he should incur in relation to his house. Thus, if two borrowers with the same incomes wished to purchase similar priced houses and yet one had a profit from an existing house while the other was a first-time buyer, the latter would be entitled to a larger loan, despite the fact that this involved a greater risk to the lending institution which, by definition, did not have a past repayment record for the first-time buyer. In the more free-market, less paternalistic atmosphere of the mid-1980s, such restraints on the borrower's freedom of action have become less common, and he is now able to decide the level of debt which is appropriate to his circumstances.

Many borrowers are now able to utilize fully the tax relief limit following the liberalization of lending policy. If someone with a £25,000 house and a £10,000 mortgage moves to a house costing £35,000 with a £30,000 mortgage, he will leave himself with a cash sum of £10,000 which he will be able to use for non-housing purposes, even though the loan which has created the cash attracts tax relief. If, however, he remains in his existing house and merely increases his existing mortgage to £20,000, the extra £10,000 of borrowing will not be eligible for tax relief, even though the equity withdrawn and the cash sum is the same. The need to move house to exploit the tax relief limit may have been a factor in explaining the large upsurge in the number of transactions in the 1980s.

Official concern over the level of equity withdrawal taking place on moving house led to a letter sent by the Bank of England to banks and by the Treasury to building societies in January 1982. The letter asked that on moving house lenders should ensure that 'the bulk of the unencumbered proceeds' of the sale should be applied to the purchase of the new dwelling. In practice this policy proved difficult to implement at a time of mortgage market liberalization. Some lending institutions began to set branch managers lending targets, rather than restricting them with quotas, and it was relatively easy to turn a blind eye to official regulations if this meant that targets would then be attained. It does seem clear that while the death of owner-occupiers will lead to a steady trend increase in equity withdrawal as the proportion of old people that die as owner-occupiers increases, it is likely that the main cause of the sharp increase in equity withdrawal in the early 1980s was due to the greater competition to obtain mortgage business.

While the expansion of tax relief consequent on the increase in (one type of) equity withdrawal has generally been deprecated by economists, it is not so clear that equity withdrawal *per se* has had deleterious effects on the economy. The Wilson Report, for example, drew attention to the extent to which small businesses were financed by the sale of inherited owner-occupied houses. An overall judgement is difficult to make because without a very detailed study of individual cases it is impossible to work out how funds released by equity withdrawal are spent. In the case of funds released by a death, a high proportion are likely to be invested because they will be received at a time when people are anxious to build up financial assets in anticipation of retirement. Some funds may be spent on items of consumption, which may have a beneficial impact on output if spent on domestically produced goods, or an adverse impact on the balance of payments if used to purchase overseas goods.

Conclusion

This chapter has examined three different, but related, concepts. The conclusions drawn are, in brief, as follows:

(1) Britain has devoted a relatively small proportion of her real resources to producing houses in recent years.
(2) Nevertheless, there has been a large increase in the flow of funds financing the exchange of existing housing.
(3) A relatively high proportion of these funds have 'leaked' from the housing market and possibly financed the output of other real resources in the economy.

It is clear that it is not possible to hold the view that housing has taken an undue proportion of available resources, while simultaneously believing that equity withdrawal involves an improper use of resources. It does seem likely that in the future house construction will decline, and equity withdrawal will increase to an extent that will put further pressure on the current arrangements for tax relief.

12 Housing Subsidies

Chapter 7 briefly explained the legislative and fiscal framework within which the mortgage market operates. This chapter is concerned with the economic impact of tax and other benefits which owner-occupiers receive, and also compares the relative positions of owner-occupiers and tenants. The government subsidies to each sector are dealt with first, a comparative study follows and finally there is a discussion on the effect of ending tax relief on mortgage interest.

An Overview

This chapter analyses subsidies by reference to tenure, but it is helpful initially to describe briefly the position as it affects various income groups:

(1) People who are unemployed have all of their housing costs paid if they are tenants, and if they are owner-occupiers they are eligible to have mortgage interest payments met, together with an allowance towards insurance and repairs.
(2) Low-income tenants qualify for housing benefit and pay little or no rent. Low-income owner-occupiers receive benefit only in the form of tax relief on mortgage interest. Low-income earners are therefore better off as tenants than owner-occupiers.
(3) At a level of income where housing benefit is no longer applicable, and this will depend both on family circumstances and the rent payable, the tenant benefits only by means of the general subsidy to local authority housing if they are a public sector tenant, and do not benefit at all if they are a private sector tenant. The level of general subsidy differs between local authorities and some no longer subsidize rents at all. Higher-income earners benefit through tax relief, the amount of their tax relief depending on the size of their mortgage, the rate of interest payable and also their marginal tax rate.

Generally, the position is that poorer people benefit financially by being tenants and better off people benefit financially by being owner-occupiers. This situation has major social and housing market implications.

Subsidies to Tenants

In the past, council housing has been very heavily subsidized. Rents have been held at an artificially low level, the cost being met both through rates and Exchequer subsidies. These general subsidies reached a peak in 1980–1 at nearly £2,500 million, or £310 per council dwelling. Since that time, the government has sharply cut back general subsidies with the figure more than halving to £1,190 million in 1985–6, an average of £200 per dwelling. This average does, of course, conceal very wide variations. The financing of local authority housing is such that some councils, particularly those with a low level of building in recent years, are not eligible for any Exchequer subsidy. Local authorities are free to use rate fund subsidies if they wish and policies differ sharply between authorities in this respect. The position is illustrated in Table 12.1, which shows the aggregate local authority housing revenue account for 1984–5.

Table 12.1 *Local Authority Housing Revenue Account, 1984–5*

Expenditure	*£m*	*Income*	*£m*
Supervision and management	912	Gross rent	3,413
Repairs and maintenance	1,254	Interest from sales	502
Interest payments	2,493	Other rents and income	379
Debt repayments	359	Exchequer subsidy	393
Other	117	Rate fund contributions	486
Transfer to rate fund	38		
Total	5,173	Total	5,173

Source: Treasury, 1986, Table 3.9.14.

The table shows that there was a transfer to the rate fund of £38 million by those councils running their council housing at a profit, but this was more than matched by rate fund contributions of £486 million. The Exchequer subsidy was £393 million. Whether or not a local authority tenant benefits from a general public subsidy therefore depends on the financial position of the local authority and the policy of that authority.

It can be argued that this historic cost method of accounting is inappropriate and that it is more logical to contrast the rents actually charged with the rents which would prevail in a free market. The difficulty of doing this is that there is no accepted method of measuring free-market rents. The historic cost method also enables reasonable comparisons to be made between local authority housing and owner-occupation.

Private sector tenants do not benefit in any way through local authority rate fund or central Exchequer subsidies. However, some such tenants have their rents at a controlled level which is well below the level which would prevail in the free market. These tenants, quite fortuitously, can be considered as being subsidized by their landlords.

For many years, many local authorities operated a rent rebate scheme by which low-income tenants were eligible for a rebate of part or all of their rent depending on the level of that rent and on their income. A national rent rebate and allowance scheme was then introduced, and from 1983 this was replaced by housing benefit. Local authorities are responsible for the administration of housing benefit. This can be subdivided into two categories.

The first is certified housing benefit. This is so named because householders who qualify for supplementary benefit are eligible for a certificate of entitlement to housing benefit from the Department of Health and Social Security. Householders on certificated benefit have all of their housing costs met, including rent, rates and insurance. Effectively, of course, maintenance and repairs are also met as these are part of the rent.

The second category is standard housing benefit. This is available for low-income people who do not qualify for supplementary benefit. It is assessed on the basis of the applicant's income in relation to a 'needs allowance'. If the applicant's income is equal to his needs allowance then he receives 60 per cent of eligible rent or rates as benefit. If income exceeds the needs allowance then benefit is reduced, and if income is less than the needs allowance then benefit is increased. As a household's income increases then in addition to normal tax payments there is also a substantial loss of housing benefit.

Housing benefit applies a substantial way up the income scale. In fact, some 55 per cent of the gross rent payable to local authorities is met by housing benefit. In 1985–6 the rent element of housing benefit was estimated at £2,290 million, or £380 per local authority dwelling. If this is added to the general subsidy of £200 per dwelling the average total subsidy was £580 per dwelling. However, it must be stressed that this average can be misleading. The subsidies received by local authority tenants range from more than £2,000 for some tenants living in fairly high rental units, but paying no rent, to nothing for many higher-income tenants. Very few tenants receive a subsidy around the average.

The reduction in Exchequer and rate fund subsidies over the past few years has in fact largely been counteracted by the increase in housing benefit. To the extent that general subsidies are reduced, then rents are increased and automatically housing benefit is also increased.

The present position is regarded by many as being unsatisfactory and leads to problems within the local authority sector:

(1) As many tenants pay no rents, effectively they have an infinite demand for housing which can never possibly be met.
(2) Rents cannot perform their economic function of rationing the available accommodation.
(3) Housing benefit contributes to the poverty trap by which low-income earners can actually suffer a reduction in living standards as their incomes increase because of taxation and the loss of housing benefit.

Subsidies to Owner-Occupiers

If the historic cost method is appropriate for measuring subsidies to local authority tenants, then it is appropriate to measure subsidies to owner-occupiers through the loss of taxation as a result of tax relief on mortgage interest. The method by which tax relief is given was explained in Chapter 7. Broadly speaking, interest on loans for house purchase or improvement up to £30,000 qualifies for tax relief at the borrower's highest marginal rate of tax. For most people this means a 29 per cent tax rate, but for some borrowers relief is available at the maximum income tax rate, currently 60 per cent. For most borrowers, relief is given through the mortgage interest relief at source system (MIRAS), which means they pay a reduced rate to the lender. However, the method of granting tax relief is largely irrelevant to the total amount.

The amount of tax relief which an individual obtains depends on the size of his loan, the rate of interest on that loan and his tax rate. On average, high-income earners tend to have larger loans than those on lower incomes. However, it is also the case that recent purchasers have higher mortgage loans than older purchasers, and the £30,000 limit now affects a large number of new loans. It is also necessary to look at the position of an individual over his whole period as an owner-occupier. A tenant, for example, is likely to receive roughly the same level of subsidy each year if his circumstances remain unchanged. In other words, if a tenant is permanently unemployed then he will receive housing benefit each year to meet all of his housing costs. However, an owner-occupier is in a different position. Tax relief will be highest initially as soon as a loan is taken out. It may then increase slightly if the borrower moves to a higher tax bracket, but, generally, it will run down as the mortgage loan is paid off, and in relation to other owner-occupiers the reduction will be even greater because of inflation. Thus what was a large loan ten years ago will now be a small loan. After a time, of course, the mortgage loan is paid off entirely and, indeed, 40 per cent of owner-occupied houses are mortgage free. It is therefore necessary to look at the position over the entire period of owner-occupation rather than at any one time.

Similarly, the total amount of tax relief depends on:

(1) The average size of loans. Obviously this increases year by year, although the £30,000 limit should begin to reduce the rate of increase of tax relieved debt in due course.
(2) The average liability to tax. Higher rate relief accounts for a comparatively small proportion, perhaps only 10 per cent, of total tax relief. If the higher rates of tax are increased, however, or thresholds reduced, then higher rate relief could increase quite considerably.
(3) In the 1986 budget the basic rate was reduced from 30 to 29 per cent

and this meant, in round terms, a 3 per cent reduction in total tax relief and also in the tax relief obtained by individual owner-occupiers.

(4) The mortgage rate. Obviously the higher the mortgage rate the greater the amount of tax relief.

(5) The number of owner-occupied houses.

The amount of tax foregone through the existence of tax relief has, in fact, been rising sharply in recent years. The total increased from £1,639 million in 1979–80 to £2,456 million in 1982–3 and an estimated £4,750 million in 1985–6. (It should be noted that these figures are based on the unlikely assumption that there would be no change in taxpayers' behaviour if relief did not exist.) This represented an increase from £140 per dwelling to £200 and £350. The increase in the amount per dwelling is largely explained by people taking out larger mortgage loans, together with a general increase in interest rates over this period.

Having explained the tax relief position, it is necessary to consider some of the anomalies which arise from treating tax relief on mortgage interest as a subsidy. It may seem to be apparent, for example, that higher rate taxpayers receive a greater subsidy than basic rate taxpayers. It is true that they obtain more tax relief, but one can argue that this needs to be balanced against the fact that they pay higher tax on investment income. Take, for example, a person subject to the basic rate of tax who has a £20,000 mortgage, and £20,000 of savings. Broadly speaking, the tax charged on the interest on the savings will basically balance the tax relief on mortgage interest. If this person now becomes liable to the 50 per cent rate of tax, then both tax relief and tax charged increase proportionately. (While this is undoubtedly true, it might also be noted that higher rate taxpayers are, in effect, able to escape the higher rates of tax on investment income by using tax sheltered instruments such as national savings certificates and low coupon or index-linked gilts.) Similarly, an increase in building society mortgage interest rates does not generally involve the government in greater net expenditure on tax relief because it is generally matched by an increase in income tax on interest paid to building society investors.

It is also necessary to consider other forms of tax relief for which owner-occupiers qualify. Some would argue that owner-occupiers are subsidized not through tax relief on mortgage interest, but rather through the absence of a tax on imputed rental income. There is much logic in looking at the position in this way, but it is unappealing to most people who cannot grasp the concept of notional rental income. Comparison with council housing has either to be on this basis, in which case council tenants would be deemed to be subsidized by the difference between their actual rents and market rents, or by the method used in this book and, more commonly, by a comparison of historic cost subsidies with actual tax relief on mortgage interest. It is not, of course, valid to argue that owner-occupiers benefit both through mortgage tax relief and through the absence of a tax on imputed rental income.

Owner-occupiers also benefit in that owner-occupied housing is exempt from capital gains tax. The annual public expenditure White Papers show a huge value for this exemption, of some £2,500 million a year. However, it must be questioned whether this figure is valid. It ignores the annual exemption, currently of £6,100, and also roll-over relief which is normally available where someone sells one asset and purchases another. Also, it is certain that owner-occupied housing now enjoys a less favoured tax status in relation to capital gains than in the 1970s. Then, with inflation running at a high level and capital gains tax being imposed on nominal capital gains, owner-occupied housing was one of the few ways in which an individual could protect the real value of his savings. Now, however, inflation has been reduced to a very low level and capital gains tax generally has been index-linked. There are also instruments such as low coupon and index-linked gilts which enable individuals to obtain tax-free capitals gains. If all of these factors are taken together, it can be argued that in no material extent does owner-occupied housing benefit from exemption from a tax which is hardly ever levied on individuals. If the tax was levied then there would be such a huge change in behaviour that any figure currently given for the cost of exemptions would be meaningless.

Before leaving the question of tax relief on mortgage interest, it is necessary to look at the impact of this tax to see whether it does benefit owner-occupiers by as much as appears from examination of the crude figures. In the case of local authority housing, the effect of subsidies is to cause a shortage and therefore queues. Owner-occupied housing, however, is a free market. A subsidy given to a consumer in a free market normally works its way through to the producer. For most of the 1970s and in the early 1980s the mortgage rate was held below a market clearing level, so it could be argued that those receiving tax relief did actually benefit from it. Now, however, the mortgage rate is set at a market clearing level. Arguably, that market clearing level is where it is partly because of the existence of tax relief. Certainly, the mortgage market has become very attractive to institutional investors who see the opportunity of obtaining a higher return than they can obtain from alternative investments.

To some extent, tax relief might also feed through to the suppliers of mortgage funds, the financial institutions, who obtain a higher net income for themselves than they could obtain if tax relief did not exist. (It is significant in this respect that the advent of the free market has led to a squeezing of building society margins on mortgage business.) Further down the chain, tax relief may also benefit those originally providing funds, such as building society investors, who are obtaining a higher return on their savings because tax relief enables higher mortgage rates to be charged. Finally, tax relief can feed through to some extent to the suppliers of housing, and ultimately to the owners of land as this is the fixed resource.

A detailed examination of these factors cannot be considered in this book and it is sufficient to note that the position of who actually benefits from mortgage tax relief is far from clear.

Before leaving subsidies available to owner-occupiers, it should be noted that the poorest owner-occupiers, those who are unemployed, are eligible for supplementary benefit to meet their mortgage interest payments. The total amount of this benefit is quite modest, perhaps only £300 million a year, but it represents a substantial benefit to those who receive it. It has no overall implications for the balance of benefit between owner-occupiers and tenants, but it is important in terms of the housing market because without this the level of arrears and possessions would probably be very much higher.

The Comparative Position

Notwithstanding the qualifications that have been made in this chapter, it is interesting to examine the relative subsidy levels between owner-occupiers and tenants. The correct way of producing the figures is open to debate. What follows is an analysis of the total tax relief and supplementary benefit available to owner-occupiers together with total public sector subsidies in the form of Exchequer and rate fund contributions and housing benefit. The figures are shown in Table 12.2. The table shows the very rapid increase in subsidies to owner-occupiers from 1980–1 to 1985–6, although on present trends there should be a reduction in 1986–7 because of lower mortgage

Table 12.2 *Housing Subsidies, Great Britain, 1980/1–1985/6*

Year	*Tax relief, option mortgage subsidy and Supplementary Benefit for Mortgage Interest*		*Subsidies to public sector tenants*			
			Exchequer and rate fund contributions	*Housing benefit for rent*	*Total*	
	£m	*£ per owner-occupied dwelling*	*£m*	*£m*	*Amount £m*	*£ per dwelling*
1980–1	2,250	190	2,450			
1981–2	2,400	200	1,860			
1982–3	2,550	200	1,410			
1983–4	2,950	230	1,200	1,980	3,180	520
1984–5	3,700	280	1,210	2,150	3,360	550
1985–6	4,900	360	1,190	2,290	3,480	580

Note: Figures for 1983–4 are taken from CSO, 1986c. Figures for other years have been provided by DoE. 1985–6 figures are provisional.

rates. The table also shows the sharp reduction in Exchequer and rate fund contributions for public sector tenants. Unfortunately, comparable figures for housing benefit are not available before 1983–4. It will be noted that the total benefit per dwelling for local authority tenants seems to have been rising rapidly compared with the total amount of benefit. This is because the number of local authority tenants has been declining as a result of sales of local authority dwellings.

The table shows that for 1985–6 the average subsidy per owner-occupier was £360 and the average subsidy per public sector tenant was £580. However, over the last few years, subsidies to owner-occupiers have been increasing more rapidly than subsidies to tenants. Again, it must be stressed that the comparison of broad averages is of little help. The general position of greater benefits being received by poor people if they are tenants, and by better-off people if they are owner-occupiers, remains.

The Political Debate on Tax Relief

Housing finance has, for many years, been the subject of intense political discussion. Traditionally, the Labour party has been seen as favouring council housing, while the Conservative party has favoured owner-occupation. Many Labour local authorities have, for example, tried to keep local authority rents as low as possible and have opposed sales of local authority dwellings.

On tax relief various arguments have been put forward as to why it should be reduced. At the one extreme is the argument that tax relief, like any other subsidy, is inherently bad, distorting the market and probably benefiting those whom it is not intended to benefit. This argument is sometimes expressed by the free-market wing of the Conservative party.

At the other extreme, it is argued that tax relief predominantly benefits the better off people and that this is inherently undesirable. Moreover, there has been a sharp reduction in council house subsidies (especially if, as is often done, housing benefit is ignored) in relation to tax relief and it is argued that this is inequitable.

In between these two rather political arguments there is also the argument that the entire housing finance system is unsatisfactory, forcing lower-income people into council housing and higher-income people into owner-occupation. In the council sector the effect is queues and a supplier of housing unresponsive to consumer demand. In the owner-occupied sector, the effect is higher prices and interest rates, and an artificial encouragement of mortgage borrowing to finance house purchase or improvements. This latter, more rational, argument has tended to gain ground at the expense of the more political arguments over the past few years, and arguably there is now a fair consensus among housing experts that the entire housing finance system needs to be reshaped such that the assistance which people get depends on their circumstances and not on their tenure.

This philosophy came through strongly in the report of the Committee of Inquiry into housing established by the National Federation of Housing Associations and chaired by the Duke of Edinburgh. The report of this committee, published in 1985, called for the gradual withdrawal of all existing housing subsidies and their replacement by a universal housing allowance.

While the intellectual argument for a reshaping of the housing finance system has gained ground, there does not seem to exist the political will for any action to be taken. The Conservative government in 1983 increased the tax relief ceiling from £25,000 to £30,000 against the opinion of the majority of housing analysts, and the government has frequently volunteered the fact that it fully supports the continuation of mortgage tax relief. For any party to suggest a reduction in tax relief is to invite strong criticism from the popular press, and it is clear that the general perception is now that politically it is impossible to reduce either the tax relief ceiling or the rate at which relief is given. In 1985, the Labour party firmly committed itself to maintenance of tax relief at the basic rate and even put forward an increase in the £30,000 ceiling. The Alliance parties are similarly committed to basic rate relief. However, neither Labour nor the Alliance parties are committed to maintaining relief at above the basic rate and arguably the Conservative government could, if it wished, abolish higher rate relief without seeming to go back on its own pledges.

In effect, the political argument on tax relief is over. Prior to any election, one party will allege that another is planning to cut back tax relief, and for electoral reasons the party so accused will immediately have to deny any such intention. A pledge as open as one to maintain mortgage tax relief cannot easily be broken. It follows that the expectation must be that tax relief will remain at its present form, although the abolition or reduction of higher rate relief cannot be ruled out.

The Effect of Abolishing Tax Relief

However, it is helpful to consider what the effect might be if, for any reason, mortgage tax relief was abolished. The extent of the effects would obviously be influenced by the time scale over which any reduction occurred. The consequences of abolition stem entirely from one key factor: the cost of borrowing up to £30,000 to finance house purchase would be increased by at least two-fifths. At present, for example, with a mortgage rate of 11 per cent and tax relief available at 29 per cent a borrower is effectively paying a net rate of 7.81 per cent. If tax relief was abolished the gross rate of 11 per cent would be payable, an increase of 41 per cent. For a borrower qualifying for

50 per cent tax relief, the increase in the cost of the mortgage would be 100 per cent. For a 75 per cent average advance with MIRAS, the basic rate taxpayer would face a 23 per cent increase in the cost of housing if tax relief were abolished. Inevitably increases in the price of mortgages of this extent, even if phased over a period of years, would have major effects. These effects can be summarized as follows:

(1) House prices would probably fall in real terms and, possibly, depending on the rate of inflation, in nominal terms as well. Land prices would also fall.
(2) Housebuilders would suffer considerably both through a reduced value of their land and a fall in the price of housing relative to their costs.
(3) A consequence of (1) and (2) could be a slump in the housing market as that investment demand for housing which still exists disappears. The position of the Netherlands is relevant in this respect. From 1979 to 1981 there was discussion about limiting tax relief. In the event, total tax deductability of mortgage interest was limited only slightly. The discussion alone, however, is considered to have contributed to a housing slump. The number of houses built for owner-occupation nearly halved between 1980 and 1982, house prices fell by 16 per cent and mortgage lenders were placed in severe financial difficulty.
(4) The demand for mortgage finance would fall much more sharply than the demand for owner-occupied housing because the relative increase in costs would be greater. People would borrow only if they had no other source of finance, whereas at present it is beneficial for most people to borrow on mortgage to finance house purchase rather than to run down savings.
(5) Gross mortgage rates would be reduced to take account of reduced demand. Correspondingly, rates to investors would also have to be reduced.
(6) The above two factors would mean a significant reduction in the rate of growth of building societies.
(7) The demand for rented housing would rise. There would be less incentive for council tenants to become owner-occupiers. Given supply constraints, for example, the rent acts, the price of private rented housing would increase.

It is difficult to apportion the effects between these various factors. However, it seems probable that much of the initial impact would be on the mortgage rate with the impact on housing variables taking some time to feed through. The main losers from any reduction in tax relief, besides borrowers with mortgage loans of £30,000 or more, would be the suppliers of mortgage finance. As building societies have 80 per cent of their assets in the form of mortgage loans, they would be most seriously affected.

Conclusion

The most that can be said for the recent debate on housing subsidies is that the issues are now much better understood. The arbitrary nature of the housing finance system and the unintended effects on supply and demand are better appreciated than they were previously. This is not to say, however, that there is likely to be any serious attempt to tackle the problem. Any attempt to reduce mortgage tax relief is deemed to be politically unacceptable and equally any attempt to reduce the impact of housing benefit is seen as being an attack on the poor. In the circumstances it seems that the country is faced with a continuation of the present unsatisfactory position which will inevitably contribute further to the polarization of the housing tenures, with all but the poorest people becoming owner-occupiers and local authority housing increasingly being reserved for the poorest sections of the community with the resultant social problems which that entails.

13 The Internationalization of Housing Finance

Housing finance is provided largely on a domestic basis, that is, only locally based institutions provide loans. Indeed, in many countries, housing finance institutions operate within much smaller geographical areas, for example, states or provinces. There has recently been much interest in the internationalization of housing finance, particularly within the United Kingdom because of the country's membership of the European Community. Also, the financial markets generally are being internationalized and housing finance institutions now have the opportunity to obtain funds relatively cheaply from the international capital markets.

Housing Finance as a Tradeable Commodity

Most physical commodities are now traded across international frontiers. International trade increases economic welfare generally, as countries benefit from their comparative advantage in producing certain commodities. It is also fairly easy to trade a tangible good, and often the ultimate consumer may have no idea of where the good was produced. Services, however, tend to be less tradeable because of their very nature, often requiring a physical presence in the market where the service is being sold. Some services, for example, restaurants, are strictly local and almost by definition can have no international context. Where, however, an intangible product such as a financial service is provided, there is obviously scope for this to be provided across national frontiers. The finance of industry and commerce is obviously an international service. As goods are traded across national frontiers, so it is necessary for the accompanying financial services to be provided on an international basis. The rapid expansion in trade since the Second World War helps to explain the internationalization of banking. Even comparatively small domestic banks need to have an international presence so as to satisfy the trade and foreign currency requirements of their customers. Those banks which are not able to have direct representation abroad may do so through linking with another bank, or through membership of a central giro organization. This is true, for example, of the co-operative banks and savings banks in West Germany.

There are few such pressures for the internationalization of housing finance. This is a service which is provided only to people and not to companies, and very few people have homes or businesses in more than one country at a time. Individuals do, of course, require financial services in respect of foreign travel and expect these services to be provided by their domestic institutions. However, borrowing to purchase a house in another country implies living in that country and almost certainly will involve a complete break with existing financial institutions.

There is, therefore, no great demand for institutions in one country to provide housing finance loans in another. Obviously, people do move from country to country and some may expect the financial institutions in the country they are leaving to help them with the loan to buy a house if indeed it is their intention to buy. Banks are generally well placed to assist here because they are international organizations and will be able to arrange a housing finance loan in another country even if they cannot provide the loan themselves.

Not only is there little demand for housing finance loans to be provided across national frontiers, but the difficulties of so doing are immense. By its very nature, a housing finance loan is likely to be secured on property. Land and mortgage law differ from country to country and the procedures that have to be gone through to make a loan in Britain are quite different from those applying in France, Germany, Italy or Spain. The administrative procedures also differ from country to country as do the tax regulations applying to the house purchase process and to tax relief on mortgage interest. Procedures for taking possession of a security also differ. In short, it is not possible for an institution in one country to simply use its existing procedures to make housing finance loans in another country. Almost certainly, it would be necessary to work through local institutions, or to employ locally based staff. Where housing finance institutions obtain their funds from retail deposits, then this would also present a problem to domestically based organizations. There are both legal and marketing obstacles to setting up a retail banking operation in any other country.

Some housing finance systems are effectively confined by national laws to their country of origin only. This is true of the *Bausparkasse* system operated in West Germany and Austria. Through this system, individuals can obtain a below-market rate of interest and government bonuses on their savings. Clearly the German and Austrian governments are not going to provide such bonuses for people to buy houses in other countries (although the German government does this to a limited extent for German civil servants in Brussels and Luxembourg), nor are governments of other countries going to subsidize foreign-based institutions at the expense of their own domestic institutions.

All of these factors suggest very little demand for housing finance to be provided across national frontiers and indeed this is the experience. Institutions such as British, Irish, Australian and South African building societies and American savings associations do not have any international operations. In the case of British building societies, they are unable to do so because the law confines them to lending on the security of freehold and leasehold estate which generally is not found outside the United Kingdom, although this form of tenure does exist in the Republic of Ireland. Similarly, other specialist institutions such as the German *Bausparkassen* operate within national frontiers except for very limited amount of activity for their members who work abroad for a short time. Mortgage banks, by the nature of their operation, relying on wholesale fund raising, are better placed for international operations, but again the specialist mortgage banks operate almost entirely within national frontiers.

The only financial institutions which do provide housing finance in more than one country are the large commercial banks, a number of which seek to provide a retail banking service as well as a commercial banking service in more than one country. The largest bank in the world, Citibank, for example, has made no secret of its ambition to become a global retail bank. Housing finance is an essential part of the retail banking service, hence Citibank is involved in providing housing finance loans in a number of countries. In addition to being a large lender in the United States, it is probably one of the largest twenty lenders in Britain through its subsidiary, Citibank Savings; it owns a mortgage bank in Spain and a building society in Australia; and it is involved in housing finance in a number of other countries as well. Among other American banks which are active in the housing finance market in Britain are Bank of America, Chemical Bank, Security Pacific and Chase Manhattan. The major British banks have a limited involvement in housing finance in the USA and other countries. Many of the other leading international banks, however, do not embrace retail activities in their international operations. Britain is perhaps more insulated than most countries to the threat of foreign invasion of the retail banking market simply because of the small number of British banks and the reluctance of the Bank of England to allow these banks to be taken over by foreign institutions. The large Japanese banks, the five largest of which are among the ten largest banks in the world, are now developing their international business and most have purchased quite significant American banks. However, there is not the same opportunity for them to purchase banks in the United Kingdom.

Fund Raising on an International Basis

Although the provision of housing finance loans remains within the province of domestic institutions, the funding of those loans is increasingly being done on an international basis. This is not a reflection of anything peculiar to housing finance, but rather results from the development of the financial markets generally. Since the mid-1960s, and particularly since the mid-1970s, the financial markets have become internationalized. Governments have gradually removed exchange controls and barriers to raising funds on an international basis, and the leading banks have responded by developing instruments which allow funds to be obtained at the lowest cost from anywhere in the world.

The major development has, of course, been the Eurodollar market. This is a market for dollar denominated deposits outside the United States. A combination of tax and regulatory reasons led to the initial growth of the Eurodollar market, and it has been used mainly by American institutions to obtain financing more cheaply than they can obtain on the domestic market, in particular for their international activities. The market has since broadened and is now used by a variety of sovereign states, industrial and commercial countries and financial institutions to raise funds at rates of interest only a fraction over money market rates. The traditional Eurobond instrument was denominated in dollars and carried a fixed rate of interest. The borrowers were American companies and the purchasers were institutional investors throughout the world which wanted dollar denominated assets. As the market has strengthened, so other instruments have become available. Particularly important has been the floating rate note, whereby funds can be raised which carry a rate of interest which floats according to the London interbank offered rate or some other money market rate. This instrument is obviously much more attractive to housing finance institutions which lend with variable rates, such as British building societies, than are fixed rate borrowings. Funds can also be raised in currencies other than dollars and there is now quite a large sterling Eurobond market.

A more recent development has been the introduction of swap techniques. These sophisticated instruments allow funds to be raised at low rates of interest by using the comparative advantage of two institutions. For example, one institution may be able to raise funds cheaply in sterling while another can raise funds cheaply in dollars. The institution which can raise funds in dollars may want sterling funds and vice versa. It can make sense for the institutions to raise the funds they need in their domestic currency and then swap them for the other's funds. Swaps can also be arranged between fixed rate and floating rate instruments. In practice, most swaps are between an institution which wishes to borrow money, and a counter-party in the form of an international bank which takes the risk itself, although obviously it will seek to lay it off through another swap arrangement. A high proportion of the Eurobond fundings are now on the swap basis.

The American housing finance institutions have made the greatest use of the Eurobond market. They had the advantage in that their secondary market instruments carry government guarantees through the Federal Home Loan Mortgage Corporation, the Federal National Mortgage Association or the Government National Mortgage Association. Effectively, the timely payment of principal and interest is guaranteed by the federal government. This has made securities backed by mortgages an attractive instrument to hold for international investors. The American federal government agencies have themselves raised funds on the Eurobond market, on the strength of the faith and credit of the US government which backs them.

The French semi-government mortgage bank, the Crédit Foncier, has also raised funds extensively on the Eurobond market. Again, it has the full backing of the government of France, and to the investor this is the security which is offered rather than the security of the institution itself or of the mortgage loans which it is making. The Crédit Foncier has made particular use of the swap market, raising funds in Japanese yen, and in the European currency unit, with the proceeds being swapped into French francs.

The use which can be made of the international capital markets is well illustrated by the position of British building societies. They were not able to tap these markets at all until a change in tax legislation enabled them to pay interest gross on Eurobonds. Effectively, societies were allowed to issue Eurobonds from October 1985. Within six months, nearly £2 billion had been raised by eleven building societies at a marginal rate of interest perhaps 1 per cent less than traditional retail funds. The borrowings have a maturity of between five and fifteen years, and their variable rate nature means they are ideally matched to societies' long-term variable rate mortgage loans. Societies have raised these funds on an entirely unsecured basis. Their mutual nature means that they offer exceptionally good security to unsecured creditors in that their shareholders, who provide most of the funds, rank behind unsecured lenders and other creditors. From March 1986, societies were able to use the swap market and a number of swap deals have subsequently been done.

Conclusion

Housing finance will remain a service which is provided largely on a domestic basis. That is, loans will be made by institutions based in the country in which the property is situated. The housing finance industry will, however, be internationalized through two other forces:

(1) As the big commercial banks become retail banks in more than one country, so they will also become providers of housing finance in more than one country and will seek to use techniques which are tried and tested in their domestic market in foreign markets.

(2) Fund raising will increasingly be on an international basis using the international capital markets. The major securities houses have an important role to play here.

PART V

The Future

14 Future Trends in Owner-Occupation and Housing Finance

The most comprehensive attempt to make forward projections of housing demand and the finance needed to meet that demand was made by the Department of the Environment (1977) in the mid-1970s as part of a review of housing policy. The resultant Green Paper, in particular its three-part technical volume, established a framework within which trends could be measured and, for a number of variables, provided for the first time a reliable base of statistical data. The technical volume included a detailed forecast of housing prospects in the medium term, the demand for owner-occupied housing and a projection of the demand for building society advances.

Since 1977 The Building Societies Association has produced two reports on future trends in the housing and housing finance markets. The first (1979) used a broadly similar methodology to that employed in the Green Paper. The major function of the report was to estimate the future demand for housing finance and the required level of building society net receipts; the main policy conclusion was that societies should move to a situation in which their interest rates were competitive, and indeed the report provided the main intellectual basis for the movement towards a competitive mortgage market covered in other chapters of this book.

The second BSA report (1985b) was more theoretical than the previous document. It examined trends in the demand for owner-occupation and the consequences on the tenure distribution of the housing stock of meeting that demand, and also the resultant demand for house purchase finance.

The rest of this chapter examines the nature of the housing and housing finance markets in the remaining years of this century, but without attempting to make detailed statistical forecasts. Rather, it analyses data from two sources, the Department of the Environment's household formation forecasts to the year 2001 (Department of the Environment, 1986) and the BSA's market research into attitudes to housing tenure (Boléat, 1986), and uses conclusions from these sources to speculate on the market conditions facing housing finance institutions at the end of the century.

The Demographic Factors

It is proper to start any analysis of the demand for housing with an analysis of the demographic characteristics of the economy. This type of analysis is more important for housing than for any other good or service produced because, unlike other products, every person needs a dwelling in which to live, but generally each person only requires one dwelling.

At the very simplest level one could relate the number of people living in the country to the number of dwellings required. This would show a very slow increase in demand. In mid-1986 the UK population was estimated to be 56.5 million, having risen marginally from 55.9 million in 1971. The government's Office of Population Censuses and Surveys suggest that the population will rise to 57.7 million by 2001.

A moment's thought, however, reveals that the individual is not the basic component of housing demand. Children do not usually require their own dwelling, and husbands and wives do not generally live in separate houses. Rather, individuals live together in households and it is the number of households that is the major demographic determinant of the demand for housing.

The number of households has been rising much more rapidly than the population itself. Between 1971 and 1981, for example, the total number of households in Great Britain rose by around 6.5 per cent, compared to an increase in population of less than 1 per cent. Single-person households have become more important within the total, accounting for only 17 per cent of households in 1971 but 25 per cent in 1984. The proportion of households with a child under 15 declined during the same period from 39 per cent to 33 per cent.

For many years the Department of the Environment has made forward projections of the number of households. These projections can never be totally reliable because, although fairly firm estimates of numbers in the population over the age of 18 can be made up to eighteen years ahead, based on knowledge of the current population and well-established mortality statistics, estimates of marriage and divorce rates and the 'headship rate' (the proportion of the population that establish and head households) are rather more problematic. Nevertheless, as long as the statistics are interpreted with caution they are useful for a 'broad brush' analysis of likely future developments.

The rate of growth of the number of households is expected by the Department of the Environment to decline as the end of the century approaches. Table 14.1 shows trends in this variable since 1961 in England and Wales.

The decline in the rate of household formation reflects, but as noted earlier is not totally dependent on, population trends. A more important factor is the age structure of the population. Past changes in the birth rate mean that the numbers of people coming into the prime household formation age group (15–29 years old) will decline rapidly. In 1986 there were 13.4 million individuals within this age group in the UK, whereas by 2001 the figure is projected to be only 10.6 million. Other factors affecting the rate of

Table 14.1 *Annual Increase in Number of Households, England and Wales, 1961–2001*

Period	*Increase*	*Period*	*Increase*
1961–1971	205,000	1986–1991	170,000
1971–1981	150,000	1991–1996	110,000
1981–1986	160,000	1996–2001	55,000

Source: Department of the Environment, 1986.

household formation include the rising rate of divorce, as divorced couples typically initially establish two households, and the increasing standard of living, which enables a greater proportion of young people to establish their own household before marrying.

The projections may have implications for the number of new houses required. There are currently more dwellings than households but once second homes, unfit dwellings and those undergoing improvement are excluded from the analysis the number of dwellings falls below the number of households. The number of new dwellings completed in the 1970s and early 1980s was therefore greater than the level of household formation, although to a declining degree. In the 1971–81 period, dwelling completions in England and Wales totalled 250,000 per annum, compared to the household formation figure of 150,000 per annum shown in the table. In the 1981–6 period the respective figures were 170,000 and 160,000. It does seem likely that the level of new housebuilding will fall further towards the level of household formation during the remainder of the century, but nevertheless there are reasons for arguing that the housebuilding industry will not be so dramatically squeezed as the figures in Table 14.1 suggest. In particular, there are three factors which suggest that the existing housing stock will not be appropriate for the needs of future households: it will not match the geographic or age distribution of households, or their tenure aspirations. The next section of this chapter investigates the first of these factors.

Regional Differences

The rate of household formation is not uniform throughout the country, but varies by region, according to the existing age and sex distribution of the population, the rates of births and deaths, and trends in emigration and immigration. In 1983, for example, there were 17.3 live births per 1,000 population in Northern Ireland compared with just 11.4 in the south-west of England. Indeed, in 1983 deaths in the south-west exceeded births, reflecting the relatively large number of elderly people, but the population rose relatively strongly because while 88,000 people left the region to move to other parts of the United Kingdom, 127,000 people moved from other parts of the country to settle in the south-west. Another example emphasises the extent of the differences between the regions. In the 1971–81 period the UK population rose by just 0.1 per cent per annum, yet in East Anglia the growth rate was twelve times higher at 1.2 per cent per annum, reflecting both net migration and a very low mortality rate when adjusted for the age of the population. By contrast, in the north of England a high mortality rate, net emigration and only an average birth rate led to a reduction in population in that region in the 1970s and 1980s.

These examples of differing regional population trends introduce the possibility of there being a regional mismatch of households and available housing. Regional shifts in population can make existing houses redundant and require heavy building elsewhere. Table 14.2 shows the extent of the diversity in regional household formation expected until the end of the century.

Table 14.2 *Regional Household Projections, 1983–2001*

Region	*Increase in number of households* %
Northern	3.5
Yorkshire and Humberside	7.9
North-west	4.9
East Midlands	16.0
West Midlands	10.8
Wales	9.4
East Anglia	20.5
South-west	17.8
South-east (excluding Greater London)	18.8
Greater London	6.5
England and Wales	11.7

Source: Department of the Environment, 1986.

It is clear from the figures that the number of households is expected to rise in the south of the country far more rapidly than in the north. The three northern regions of England, the West Midlands and Wales – that is, the region to the north and west of a line joining the Bristol Channel to the Humber estuary – all have projected household growth rates of less than 11 per cent, while the two southern regions and East Anglia have growth rates in excess of 17 per cent, although the Greater London area, in common with other urban areas, shows a relatively slow growth.

At the sub-regional level the differences are even greater. The urban areas comprising the now disbanded Metropolitan Counties of Merseyside and Tyne and Wear are projected to have 1 per cent fewer households in 2001 than 1983, while the highest growth rate of any of the six former metropolitan counties is 6.6 per cent in West Yorkshire. In contrast, Buckinghamshire is expected to experience a 34 per cent increase in households, with a number of other predominantly rural, southern counties having projected growth rates in excess of 20 per cent.

These regional shifts have a number of long-term implications for housing finance institutions. First, the growth in the mortgage market is likely to be related to household growth thus placing those institutions with a bias towards the south and east in a stronger position to obtain new business than those based in the north. This has implications especially for northern-based regional building societies, but also for banks like the trustee savings banks which are under-represented in the south-east.

Secondly, house price differences between regions seem unlikely to decline. In the past, regional house price inflation rates have been broadly similar over a long run of years, although significant year by year variations have been common. However, the divergence in expected household formation rates over the next twenty years is so great that this pattern will come under pressure. A widening differential between house prices in the north and south of the country is possible given the differing patterns of demand. Whether this is to be welcomed depends on an assessment of two conflicting arguments. Some may suggest the widening house price gap will make it even more difficult for unemployed people in the north to move southwards in order to take up work. The alternative argument is that if house prices do rise more rapidly in the south this will be the inevitable consequence of the successful movement by a number of households from the north to the south. In essence, therefore, increasing differences between regional average house prices can be seen as either a factor restricting household mobility or a result of increasing household mobility. It is difficult to be sure of the relative importance of these two factors.

The third consequence for housing finance institutions is that the figures suggest some further, at least relative, decline in inner-city areas. Those households migrating from those areas are likely to be the economically active leading to an increasing concentration of the elderly and unemployed, and leaving a less hospitable environment for those building societies and other institutions concerned about the security of their loans on inner-city properties. Most importantly, existing houses in inner-city areas may be left derelict while the demand for new houses in greenfield sites increases.

The Age Structure of the Population

It was noted earlier that the numbers of the population in the 15–29 year age group would decline rapidly in the years to 2001. This is reflected in the household formation projections, which show a large decline in the number of married couple households in this age category. Table 14.3 shows the extent of the reduction.

Table 14.3 *Married Couple Households Headed by Male Aged 15–29, England, 1983–2001*

Year	*Thousands*
1983	1,180
1986	1,150
1991	1,187
1996	1,063
2001	882

Source: Department of the Environment, 1986.

The group of households examined in the table is the prime first-time buying group. In 1983 there were almost 1.2 million married couples in the 15–29 age band. The number is expected to remain more or less unchanged until 1991, but by 2001 there will be fewer than 900,000 households in this category – a decline of over a quarter in ten years. The number of single-person and single-parent households in this age category is forecast to rise very slowly over the 1983 to 1991 period and then decline in the years to 2001.

While the number of young married couples is expected to fall, the number of married couples where the male is over 30 is expected to increase so that overall the number of married couple households is projected to remain broadly constant to the year 2001. As well as married couples the Department of the Environment's forecasts identify single-parent households, single-person households and 'other' households. The most rapid growth of household type is that of single persons. The number of single person male households aged 30–44 is projected to more than double in England between 1983 and 2001, while the number of female households is expected to rise nearly two and a half times. In the 45–59 (female)/64 (male) age group the respective growth rates are 53 per cent and 43 per cent. Overall the number of households is expected to rise by 12 per cent. The growth in one-parent households is less marked but still substantial; an increase of 25 per cent is projected for this category over the 1983–2001 period.

As with geographic shifts, the implications of this change are twofold. Dealing first with housing finance institutions, it will be shown in the next section that the vast majority of young people wish to be owner-occupiers. Nevertheless the increasing level of owner-occupation (which in itself reduces the proportion of first-time buyers as more and more of those entering the housing market already own a dwelling) combined with the declining number of households in the first-time buyer group means that the overall financial sophistication of those seeking mortgages will be much greater than in the past. Increasingly, potential borrowers will already be existing borrowers and will therefore have greater knowledge of the market and be able to make a more informed judgement on the various financial packages on offer.

The second implication once again concerns the mismatch between the existing housing stock and a distribution of households that has changed since that stock was built. As the single-person and one-parent population grows there will be a demand for smaller, cheaper dwellings that suggests a further increase in the use of converted flats and new building of smaller dwellings than in the past. In fact the size of new dwellings built has declined consistently since the mid-1970s as builders have recognized this trend (although it is possible there was a slight reversal of policy in 1985).

Tenure Aspirations

Reference to tenure aspirations has already been made in this chapter when it was argued that most young people would like to become owner-occupiers. One established method of examining the demand for a product, be it soap powder, motor cars, or owner-occupied housing, is to conduct market research. The Building Societies Association, towards the end of 1985, commissioned the British Market Research Bureau (BMRB) to conduct a comprehensive review of attitudes to housing and housing tenure. About 2,500 adults were interviewed in February and March of 1986; the survey was based on a random location design.

A major question asked of respondents was: 'what is your expected housing tenure in ten years' time?' Table 14.4 shows the replies broken down by age of respondent. It can be seen that in the under 55 age group around 90 per cent of adults expect to be owner-occupiers in ten years' time. There is very little demand for council rented accommodation except in the elderly age groups, probably reflecting the current concentration of the elderly in that tenure.

If people's expectations are to be realized one solution would be a very large housebuilding programme in the private sector to enable those people currently in council dwellings to purchase homes of their own. This would leave much of the existing council stock redundant. The obvious alternative policy is to change the tenure of the existing stock. This policy has, of course, been followed since 1980 with the introduction of the 'Right to Buy'.

Table 14.4 *Expected Tenure in Ten Years' Time by Current Tenure (Percentage of Total)*

Age	*Unweighted sample*	*Owner-occupation*	*Council renting*	*Private renting*	*Don't know*
16–19	207	87 (55)	7 (33)	3	4
20–24	209	91 (52)	3 (27)	1	4
25–34	452	93 (72)	4 (21)	1	2
35–54	775	88 (74)	8 (23)	1	3
55–64	360	70 (66)	25 (31)	1	4
65+	452	54 (56)	29 (37)	5	12
Total	2,455	80 (65)	13 (28)	2	5

Source: Boléat, 1986.
Note: Figures in brackets show current tenure.

The 1986 BMRB survey took place against a background which had seen around 800,000 public sector houses sold to their tenants. Sales reached a peak in 1982 and had fallen to less than half that peak by 1986; there had been a belief that most of the dwellings that could be sold had been sold. Nevertheless, BMRB asked those who were still council tenants whether they were interested in purchasing their homes. The results are shown in Table 14.5.

Table 14.5 *Interest of Council Tenants in Purchasing Their Homes (Percentage of Heads of Households or Spouses who are Council Tenants)*

Interest	*20–24*	*25–34*	*35–54*	*55–64*	*65+*	*All*
Unweighted sample	209	452	775	360	492	
Very interested	14	22	27	12	6	16
Quite interested	24	22	19	11	9	15
Indifferent	0	2	3	7	3	3
Not very interested	20	25	21	22	18	21
Not at all interested	42	27	29	47	64	44
Don't know	0	2	1	1	0	1

Source: Boléat, 1986.

The table shows that 31 per cent of council tenants are interested in buying their homes and that interest in buying is, not surprisingly, most marked in the younger age groups. Again, not surprisingly, there was a much greater interest among those living in houses than in flats in buying. It is rather more interesting to note that although 31 per cent of tenants were interested in buying, only 15 per cent thought it was likely that they would do so. Nevertheless, 46 per cent of council tenants expect to be owner-occupiers in ten years' time. If these preferences are met, large numbers of council flats will not be required by the end of the century.

This may be a pessimistic conclusion. The earlier parts of this chapter have suggested that there may be a mismatch in the future between the type of households and the stock of dwellings available. It is perhaps rather rash to assume that existing households are perfectly matched to the existing housing stock and it is possible to envisage council flats being sold into the private sector for occupation by some of the growing single-person households identified earlier.

Conclusion

It is worth setting out in summary form the major conclusions from this analysis:

(1) The declining level of household formation and rising level of owner-occupation mean that a smaller proportion of housing finance institutions' lending will be to first-time buyers or on the security of new dwellings. To an even greater extent than currently, institutions' lending will facilitate the exchange of existing dwellings between existing owner-occupiers.

(2) As a consequence of (1), institutions will need to sell their products into an increasingly knowledgeable market. This reinforces the conclusion of Chapter 9 that inefficient institutions will find it more difficult to survive in the new market conditions.

(3) Mortgage markets in the south and east of England are likely to grow more rapidly from those in the north and west. House prices may show similar differential growth. Not only does this suggest a more rapidly expanding market in the south and east, but also a safer market as rapid house price inflation increases lenders' security and reduces the effect of lending 'errors'. Organizations lending purely on commercial grounds are likely to concentrate on the south and east. (Indeed, some of the newer institutions in the mortgage market appear to have implemented this policy already by setting minimum loan limits that make it unlikely that they will receive applications from the lower-priced areas of the country.)

(4) The increasing mismatch between the type of household in existence and the nature of the housing stock may lead to a demand for new housing greater than the level of household formation, although below today's levels.

References

Blaesser, B. W. (1981), *Clandestine Development in Colombia* (Washington: Agency for International Development).

Boléat, M. J. (1985), *National Housing Finance Systems: A Comparative Study* (Beckenham: Croom Helm/IUBSSA).

Boléat, M. J. (1986), *Housing in Britain* (London: The Building Societies Association).

BSA (1979), *Mortgage Finance in the 1980s*, Stow Report (London: The Building Societies Association).

BSA (1983), *Building Societies and the Savings Market* (London: The Building Societies Association).

BSA (1985a), *BSA Bulletin*, July, vol. 43, p. 7.

BSA (1985b), *Mortgage Finance into the 1990s* (London: The Building Societies Association).

BSA (1986a), *BSA Bulletin*, April, vol. 46.

BSA (1986b), *Building Society Fact Book 1985* (London: The Building Societies Association).

Committee to Review the Functioning of Financial Institutions (1980), *Report and Appendices*, Wilson Report (London: HMSO).

Commonwealth Banking Corporation (1985), *Annual Report 1985* (Sydney: Commonwealth Banking Corporation).

CSO (1985), *United Kingdom National Accounts* (London: HMSO).

CSO (1986a), *Financial Statistics*, April (London: HMSO).

CSO (1986b), *Economic Trends Annual Supplement* (London: HMSO).

CSO (1986c), *Financial Statistics*, February (London: HMSO).

CSO (1986d), *Social Trends*, February (London: HMSO).

Department of the Environment (1977), *Housing Policy: A Consultative Document* (London: HMSO).

Department of the Environment (1986), *1983 Based Estimates of Numbers of Households 1983–2001* (London: HMSO).

Deutsche Bundesbank (1983), 'Recent developments in building and loan association business', *Monthly Report of the Deutsche Bundesbank*, April, vol. 35, no. 4, pp. 25–33.

Deutsche Bundesbank (1986a), *Monthly Report of the Deutsche Bundesbank*, April, vol. 38, no. 4.

Deutsche Bundesbank (1986b), *Statistische Beiheft zu den Monatsberichten der Deutschen Bundesbank*, 1st series, April.

Guttentag, J. M. (1984), 'Recent changes in the primary mortgage market', *Housing Finance Review*, July (Washington: Federal Home Loan Mortgage Corporation).

HDFC (1985), *Seventh Annual Report 1983–84* (Bombay: Housing Development Finance Corporation Ltd).

HMSO (1985), *Building Societies Bill* (London: HMSO).

HM Treasury (1984), *Building Societies: A New Framework* (London: HMSO).

HM Treasury (1986), *The Government's Expenditure Plans 1986–7 to 1989–90* (London: HMSO).

Inquiry into British Housing (1985), *Report* (London: National Federation of Housing Associations).

Jaffee, D. M. (1984), 'Creative finance: measures, sources and tests', *Housing Finance Review*, January (Washington: Federal Home Loan Mortgage Corporation).

Lall, V. D. (1982), *Some Aspects of Economics of Housing in India* (New Delhi: The Times Research Federation).

Ministry of Regional Planning, Building and Urban Environment (1982), *Monograph on the Human Settlements Situation and Related Trends and Policies* (Bonn: Ministry of Regional Planning, Building and Urban Environment).

OECD (1985a), *Purchasing Power Parities and Real Expenditures in the OECD* (Paris: OECD).

OECD (1985b), *Historical Statistics 1960–1983* (Paris: OECD).

Office of Population Censuses and Surveys (1983), *Recently Moving Households* (London: HMSO).

Realkreditradet (1986), *Beretning og regnskab 1985* (Copenhagen: Realkreditradet).

Schuster, L. and Beckstrom, R. A. (1984), 'The Swiss mortgage industry', *Federal Home Loan Bank Board Journal*, March (Washington: Federal Home Loan Bank Board).

Registry of Friendly Societies (1985), *Report of the Chief Registrar 1983–84* (London: HMSO).

Shah, P. P. (1984), 'Operational problems and potential for low income lending', paper presented to Asia Housing Finance Seminar (unpublished).

Treasury (1986), *The Government's Expenditure Plans 1986–87 to 1988–89*, Vol. II, Cmnd 9702–II (London: HMSO).

UCB (1986), *Union de Crédit pour le Bâtiment, 1985* (Paris: Union de Crédit pour le Bâtiment).

USLSI (1983), *The 1982 Savers Survey* (Chicago: United States League of Savings Institutions).

Index